124 East 40th Street
New York, New York 10021

In 1782 a naturalized American of French birth essayed to describe the country of his adoption and the character of its people. His observations appeared in *Letters from an American Farmer*, one of the most delightful books published in the colonial period.

In America, Hector St. John de Crèvecoeur concluded, the Old World immigrant became a free man, a member of a new race, with a destiny dimly foreseen as "causing great changes in the world."

How did this happen? Who were the men and women who launched our nation, and what were the motivating forces of their lives and achievements? What is their message for us today?

From their own statements and other contemporary documents, Francis Bradley, a descendant of one of George Washington's officers, has prepared a fully referenced source-book of the origins and originators of The United States of America.

The publishers take pleasure in offering this volume as a public service.

THE AMERICAN PROPOSITION

THE AMERICAN PROPOSITION

A New Type of Man

By FRANCIS BRADLEY

Illustrations by
JAQUELIN TALIAFERRO SMITH

MORAL RE-ARMAMENT, INC.
New York
1977

Dedicated
to
Lee Vrooman
1897–1954
Educator—Innovator—Statesman

Long a student and lover of American history, Lee
Vrooman deserves an honored place among those
American educators whose dedication helped shape
the leadership of new national states in our time.
A graduate of the University of Maine, he worked
for many years in the Near East. He became Professor
and Dean of the International College at Ismir, Tur-
key, and a pioneer in strengthening democracy through
Moral Re-Armament. His articles on Turkish life and
history appeared in American, Turkish, Iranian and
Arabic publications. He was also co-author of several
widely used study books on America. His last work,
The Faith That Built America, inspired this writing.

Contents

Illustrations

PROLOGUE
"Novus Ordo Seclorum"
(New Order of the Ages)[1]

What then is the American, this new man? . . . He is an American who, leaving behind him all his ancient prejudices and manners, receives new ones from the new mode of life he has embraced, the new government he obeys and the new rank he holds. . . . Here individuals of all nations are melted into a new race of men, whose labors and posterity will one day cause great changes in the world. . . . The American is a new man, who acts upon new principles; he must therefore entertain new ideas and form new opinions. . . .

HECTOR ST. JOHN DE CRÈVECOEUR—1782[2]

PREFACE

If there is any period one would desire to be born in, is it not the age of Revolution; when the old and the new stand side by side and admit of being compared; when the energies of all men are searched by fear and hope; when the historic glories of the old can be compensated by the rich possibilities of the new era? This time, like all times, is a good one, if we but know what to do with it.

RALPH WALDO EMERSON—1837[1]

OUR generation has seen further advance in scientific and material development during the past half-century than in the whole of Man's previous history. Technology has shrunk our world—and perhaps our universe—into a neighborhood. The scope and pace of change outstrip our understanding and control of events.

If we are ever to master these forces, we must somehow learn from the experience of the past. For history reminds us that change is a law of life and that every step of change brings dislocations, often abrupt and painful, to contemporary living. America was born at such a period. "Truly we may say that never did men grow old in so short a time," observed Tom Paine in 1776. "We have crowded the business of an age into . . . a few months."[2]

Political and social convulsions had attended earlier western discoveries. The Reformation on the Continent and revolutions in England and later France had overturned old systems and concepts. New horizons were opening and fresh energies being released for the people of those days.

The road to America would lead not to the fabled riches

1

of "Cathay" but to a new world, where men of faith and courage could build a new society and many who had never made it in the old country would find a haven and a hope. Explorers, pilgrims, settlers, immigrants—the American venture was for many a "great and high undertaking."[3] Christopher Columbus planting the flag of Spain upon the outskirts of a great, unknown Continent believed his voyage to have been a divine mission, and looked upon himself as an example of an ordinary person used to bring about extraordinary results.[4]

America flourished. Her ideas and institutions spread across the world and drew to our shores succeeding generations of men and women seeking a better life.

Today new frontiers of space and of the spirit face us with new challenges. As America moves into her 3rd century, it is natural and fitting to recall events of our history and to look with fresh appreciation at the men and women who built our country, won her freedom and established her separate and equal status among the nations.

The purpose of this writing is not to add anything to the record, but rather to highlight some aspects of the founders' experience which could illumine our own path and strengthen our resolve. For they in no sense felt their work was finished. They had faith in the future. "Our children will be as wise as we are," Thomas Jefferson predicted, "and will establish in the fullness of time those things not yet ripe for establishment."[5]

Our founders speak to us today, and never more clearly than when we ourselves decide to catch from their hands, if we can, the torch of faith that is the heritage of every generation of Americans.

CHAPTER I

Old World Origins

I always consider the settlement of America with reverence and wonder, as the opening of a grand scheme and
design in Providence for the illumination and emancipation of mankind all over the earth.

JOHN ADAMS—1765[1]

THE Europeans who first set foot upon American soil
were inspired by a combination of motives. To early
explorers, America had been a way station to the Indies.
Imperial ambitions clashed in the widening Western Hem-
isphere. Boundless natural resources, potential markets and
elbow room soon attracted colonists. Profit was an element
in the formation of groups like the Virginia-London and
Plymouth Companies and similar organizations in France,
Holland and Sweden. Adventurers headed the procession,
and even the jails of England contributed their quota
(mostly poor debtors) of immigrants to the British colonies.

The period of discovery and settlement was above all a
time of great expectations, an age of faith, and books like
Sir Thomas More's *Utopia* raised visions of an "ideal republic" in the new lands to the west. Roman Catholic priests
accompanied the Spanish, French, and Portuguese expeditions; it was Fra Junipero Serra who built the California
missions, while Pere Marquette with other dedicated missionaries penetrated the northern forests and brought
Christianity to the Indians. Many later English settlers
came, as Governor Bradford wrote, out of a "pious and

3

religious affection and desire of propagating the gospel of our Lord Jesus Christ."[2]

The social ferment in Europe during the 16th and 17th centuries spurred emigration to the new world. Ancient principles of "Divine Right" were challenged by theories of self-government confirmed by "natural law." The Puritan movement spread over Britain and northern Europe, particularly the Netherlands and Switzerland, and democratic religious bodies multiplied in England, also in Scotland, where King James I denounced a Presbytery which "agreed with monarchy as well as God with the Devil," and threatened to "make them conform themselves" or he would "harry them out of the land."[3]

Many suffered persecution for their beliefs. In England, Puritans were summarily dismissed from their jobs and thrown into filthy jails where they caught diseases and died. During Charles II's reign, over 3,000 Quakers were imprisoned, and it was in Bedford Gaol that John Bunyan wrote his *Pilgrim's Progress*.

In those days, moreover, dissenters faced worse than imprisonment or loss of civil rights. Numbers were hanged or burned at the stake. An inscription still to be seen at Glasgow Cathedral stands as a memorial to a group of these martyrs:

> Whose bodies here interred by
> Then sacrificed to tyranny,
> To Covenants and Reformation
> Cause they adhered to their station.
> These nine with others in this year
> Whose hearts and bodies were not spared.
> Their testimonies, foes to bury
> Caused beat the drums then in great fury.[4]

On the Continent, the state of affairs was even worse. German colonists from the Rhineland had seen the country laid waste and half the population killed off in the religious wars and, in France, survivors of the Huguenot massacres scattered across Europe and America.

Hazards of the transatlantic crossing and hardships of frontier life would present no barrier to those who turned their faces toward the new Canaan. The Plymouth pilgrims setting sail for New England, after a dozen years' exile in Holland, "looked not much on those things, but lifted up their eyes to the heavens, their dearest country, and quieted their spirits."[5]

God's hand, later writers would conclude, must have been in the discovery and settlement of America at the very time when many a persecuted minority had need of such a refuge.

But America provided much more than a refuge.* To disillusioned peoples of the old world, the new settlements held the promise of a better life than men had known. For millions, America has been the fulfillment of this promise.

* The (Massachusetts) Bay Company was not a battered remnant of suffering Separatists thrown upon a rocky shore. It was an organized task force of Christians, executing a flank attack on the corruptions of Christendom. The Puritans did not flee to America. They went in order to work out that complete reformation which was not yet accomplished in England and Europe.

PERRY MILLER[6]

CHAPTER II

Charters–Compacts–Covenants

There stands the cause between God and us.
We are entered into a covenant for this work.
We have taken out a commission; the Lord
hath given us leave to draw our own articles.
                    JOHN WINTHROP—1630[1]

THE "stern and rockbound coast" sighted by the Mayflower November, 1620, lay far to the north of Virginia, where the Pilgrims had hoped to settle. It was even
further remote from the jurisdiction of London, and the
leaders of the expedition, meeting in the ship's cabin, drew
up and signed what was for all practical purposes a constitution for an independent American state.

The Mayflower pact is perhaps the first example in history of "that positive, original social compact . . . the only
legitimate source of government."[2] It embodied radical
ideas of freedom and equality which would be tested in the
new settlements. Their "body politick" was something more
than a political structure; it reflected New Testament principles. "We are knit together as a body," declared the Pilgrims writing to Sir Edwin Sandys from Holland before
the Plymouth venture, "in a most sacred bond and covenant
of the Lord." It was in this union that they held themselves
"strictly tied to all care of each other's good and of the
whole by everyone . . . mutually."[3]

Puritan pastors had envisaged a Christian Commonwealth, where self-government was to be identified with

7

submission to a higher Authority. Civil magistrates installed "by the consent and choice of the people" must be first of all "persons authorized by God."[4] The signers of the Mayflower pact recorded their purpose as nothing less than, "The glory of God and advancement of the Christian faith, and honor of our king and country."

Here was the design for "the city set upon a hill."[5] The Puritan settlements spread, and with them the "Covenant Principle." In New Hampshire towns, citizens combined to set up "such a government as shall be to our best discernment agreeable to the will of God."[6] Foundations were laid for "democratical" governments, first in Rhode Island,[7] and then in New Jersey where the Quaker proprietors would "put the power in the people."[8] Upon this same base was built the "Fundamental Orders of Connecticut,"[9] the first truly political Constitution in America, and the New England Confederation,[10] an early step toward colonial unity. A Massachusetts code of laws, significantly termed "The Body of Liberties," confirmed "rights, liberties and privileges"[11] later included in the Bill of Rights by the U.S. Constitution.

Royal charters, to be sure, had secured to British colonists and their descendants rights and "privileges of free denizens and persons native of England."[12] But England lay far away beyond the seas. Could Massachusetts citizens, for example, be bound by allegiance to British laws when they no longer lived in England? Surely not! "For the laws of the Parliament of England reach no farther."[13]

Attempts by King Charles II to strengthen the royal dominion over his subjects across the Atlantic ran up against communities of freedom-minded citizens who were opposed to his schemes and beyond reach of his control. One hundred years before Concord and Lexington, Puritan ministers had stated the colonists' conviction that when the body of the people should find their rulers "to have broken the fundamental articles of their Covenant" and violated the way of peace and happiness they were sworn to maintain, "it shall then be lawful to take up arms against them."[14]*

The seed had been sown from which would mature the ideas proclaimed in the Declaration of Independence. "The Revolution began," wrote John Adams, "as early as the first plantation of the country."[16]

* Thirteen years before the Civil War, in a paraphrase of Jefferson's familiar dictum, Abraham Lincoln declared, "Any people anywhere, being inclined and having the power, have the right to rise up and shake off the existing government and form a new one that suits them better."[15]

CHAPTER III

The Plantation Colonies

> Let us turn from hearts of stone and iron, and pray . . .
> that it would please Him to bless and water these feeble
> beginnings, and . . . so to nourish this grain of seed, that
> it may spread till all people of the earth admire the
> greatness, and seek the shades and fruit thereof.
>
> "A TRUE AND SINCERE DECLARATION"
> —Virginia-London Company, 1610[1]*

VIRGINIA was the first permanent English settlement to be
planted in North America. An eyewitness describes
the impression made upon the arrivals at the site of Jamestown on Sunday April 26, 1607, by the "fair meadows and
goodly, tall trees" and sparkling water which met their
gaze as they approached the coast. "They were ravished at
the sight thereof," he reported.

The Jamestown venture had been preceded by several
unsuccessful attempts to extend the British Empire and the
Kingdom of God on the American mainland. Sir Humphrey
Gilbert, voyaging to Newfoundland in 1583, had proclaimed his resolute purpose "to discover, possess and re-
duce into the service of God" these "remote and heathen
countries," while at the same time he warned prospective
colonists against "worldly motives of avarice and ambition."[2]

* In this remarkable document the Virginia Company struck an ecu-
menical note, calling for "a virtuous emulation between us and the
Church of Rome" in the primary aim "to recover out of the arms of
the Divell" the lost souls of the heathen natives.

Sir Humphrey was lost at sea, and his half-brother, Sir Walter Raleigh, inherited the charter he had obtained from Queen Elizabeth I, "The Virgin Queen" after whom the colony was named. The charter covered in effect all the territory of North America which the English might be able to settle and hold. Sir Walter sent two expeditions to Roanoke Island off the coast of what is now North Carolina, but the first was abandoned after two years, and the second ("The Lost Colony") disappeared and left no trace.*

Despite such failures, conditions in England encouraged emigration. The country was overpopulated, needed sources of raw materials and markets for her manufactures. A "Northwest Passage" might prove to be the long-sought route to the Indies.** Religious issues turned men's hearts and hopes to new horizons.

Interest in the western lands had been stirred by fresh discoveries and stimulated by such writers as Richard Hakluyt, the geographer and clergyman whose works were bestsellers in London at the time, who was to cherish among many honors and achievements his appointment as first Rector of the Jamestown Parish.

The Virginia-London Company was a group which had been formed for purposes of conversion, colonization and trade. In 1606, the Company sent an expedition of three small ships with 120 colonists to establish a settlement in Virginia.

Among other things, the founders of the Jamestown colony hoped to strengthen Britain in her struggle with His Catholic Majesty Philip II of Spain, and the Church of England backed the project wholeheartedly. Sermons in support of the enterprise were reprinted, and funds soon

* Virginia Dare, the first white child born in North America (Aug. 18, 1587), was the granddaughter of John White, leader of Sir Walter's second expedition.

** Sir Humphrey Gilbert had written in 1566, when he was twenty-seven years old, "A Discourse to Prove a Passage by the Northwest to Cathaia (China)."

raised to found a college near the present site of Richmond, embodying hopes of converting young Indians and educating both them and the youth of the colony.

Jamestown got off to a poor start. More than once the colony was on the point of being abandoned by disheartened survivors of the almost incredible hardships which the colonists encountered. Within two years, nine out of ten of the original settlers had died from disease, starvation, or Indian attacks. Yet fresh immigrants arrived and the colony struggled along.

The only thing that kept the Virginia colony alive through these difficult years was the vision and faith of some of its founders, well expressed in a poetical paraphrase of a Report by the Deputy-Governor in 1610:

"Be not dismayed at all
For scandall cannot doe us wrong,
God will not let us fall.
Let England knowe our willingnesse,
For that our work is good;
Wee hope to plant a nation
Where none before hath stood."

The London backers of the colony could recognize in its survival clear evidence of the Almighty's favor. In a long report, they recorded many instances of His gracious guidance and protection. "Never had any people more just cause to be grateful for God's mercies than our distressed colony,"[3] they concluded.

The Virginia colonists labored under particular handicaps. Absentee ownership of land and produce by the Company discouraged individual initiative. This was evidenced when, after five lean years, each settler was given three acres for his own use, and a ten-fold increase in the harvest was reported by the Governor, Captain John Smith.[4]

A further drawback was the absence of women. Although from the beginning the colony had included a handful of female settlers, most of these had not survived the rigors of frontier life. In 1620, the Company undertook to recruit a contingent of "young, uncorrupt maids" and ship them to Jamestown. Each girl promptly found a husband, and the colony began to take on the character of a community.

The Virginia Company charter guaranteed to the colonists and their descendants "all liberties . . . to all intents and purposes as if they had been abiding and born within this our realm of England."[5] It was not until 1619, however, that the first Popular Assembly, termed the "House of Burgesses," met in Jamestown.* For a time, moreover, the colony had been governed under military regulations repugnant to Englishmen bred up under "a government of laws, not men." The offensive ordinances were repealed, and Virginia secured under English Common Law.

Self-government in Virginia owed much to men who, although they never set foot in America, directed the affairs of the Virginia-London Company until its dissolution. Prominent among these was Sir Edwin Sandys, who initiated many of the reforms under which the Company had begun to prosper until the Indian massacre of 1622. A son of the Archbishop of Canterbury, Sandys had studied for the ministry at Oxford University and written books on religion and ecclesiastical law. As Chairman of the Company, it was he who laid down the principle that the Virginians were to "have no government put upon them save by their own consent."[6]**

The Company surrendered its charter in 1624 and Virginia became a Royal Province. Under the King's Governors, however, the House of Burgesses continued to meet until the British Parliament itself was suppressed by Charles I. Subsequently, under Cromwell's Commonwealth, Vir-

* Early Virginia electorates apparently included some fifty Poles, who were employed in the production of pitch, tar and turpentine, and a few other nationalities. Unlike the Spanish, the English did not limit the franchise to citizens of their own country.

** "Choose the Devil if you will," King James I admonished the Company, "but not Sir Edwin Sandys!"

ginia's liberties were confirmed under an agreement which recognized that her citizens were to "enjoy such freedoms and privileges as belong to the freeborn peoples of England."[7]

Profit and politics, which played their part in the settlement of Virginia, cannot obscure the primary purpose which inspired Englishmen to back the project with their money long after hope of financial return had faded. As early as 1610, the principal aim of the Virginia enterprise had been proclaimed as "the plantation of a Church of English Christians."[8] Prospectuses advertising the opportunity to advance the Kingdom of God warned "all well-affected subjects" who should "jointly take in hand this high and acceptable work" to guard against selfish motives lest a "bitter root of greedy gain" become "so settled in our hearts (as to) draw our purses from the charge."[9] Kindred instructions were sent by the Company to the Virginia House of Burgesses and Council.[10]

The first act of the first Assembly which met with the Governor in the church at Jamestown was to offer a prayer for God's guidance and His blessing upon their proceedings.[11] Subsequently, the Company took care to provide for "at least one Godly and learned minister" to be chosen by the people to serve in each borough.[12] In Anglican Virginia, as in Congregational New England, "severe and wholesome laws"[13] dealt with conversion of the Indians, made church attendance compulsory, and ruled against gambling at cards or dice. Of the early edicts passed in colonial Virginia, half, it is reckoned, were concerned with moral conduct and religious observance.

The legend that Virginia was settled by "Cavaliers" originated with the royalists, adherents of Charles II, who emigrated to America after the Civil War in England. Like the main body of English settlers, however, these represented a cross-section of British society in which could be counted chaplains of Puritan leanings. The Rev. Alexander Whitaker, for example, who converted Pocahontas, was the son of a Puritan theologian.

The story of Pocahontas, daughter of an Indian chief, and her marriage to the English settler John Rolfe, is one of the earliest American romances.* Rolfe's major contribution to Virginia, however, was his success in developing out of the Indian tobacco a product which became universally popular in Europe and provided the colony with its chief export.

Within 100 years after the founding of Jamestown, settlers had taken up most of the rich tidewater lands. The frontier moved westward and southwestward across the Allegheny Mountains, through the Shenandoah Valley, into the Carolinas. Into this new territory flowed a stream of later immigrants who included Scotch-Irish, German and other north European elements, leavening the original English population. Thomas Jefferson and Patrick Henry were among Virginia's leaders who came out of this "western" frontier.

By the middle of the 17th century, Virginia had become the wealthiest and most populous of Britain's North American colonies. She continued to furnish outstanding leadership in the early days of the Republic, and has since contributed more Presidents to the United States than any other State.

The Carolinas and Georgia were colonized by English and other Europeans, along with an increasing body of immigrants from the more thickly populated sections of other colonies, including the West Indies.

During the 16th century, Spanish and French explorers had touched on the coast north of Florida and settlements

* Writing to Governor Dale to request his "grave and mature judgement" upon an "undertaking of so mightie a matter," Rolfe declared he was "no way led . . . with the unbridled desire of carnall affection" but for "the good of this plantation, for the honor of our countrie, for the glory of God, for my owne salvation, and for the converting to the true knowledge of God and Jesus Christ"[14] of his intended bride.

had been attempted, but none survived. Early English efforts under Sir Walter Raleigh, after whom the North Carolina State Capital was to be named, proved no more successful, and it was not until 1660 that immigrants from Virginia, many of them poor farmers forced out by low prices for tobacco and the spread of slavery, began to arrive in North Carolina.

In 1663 King Charles II gave grants of territory in South Carolina to English proprietors, who procured a charter, named their grant after the King, and launched a publicity campaign in Britain to attract settlers. Two years later the King extended his grant to include North Carolina and in 1670 a settlement was established at Albemarle Point. To the south, a British expedition founded a town near the present site of Charleston.*

Intermittent conflicts with Spanish, French, Indians, and pirates failed to discourage immigration to the Carolinas. In an effort to draw emigrants from the Continent, the proprietors had issued a "declaration and proposal," based upon the charter, that the colonists enjoy "freedom and liberty of conscience of all religious and spiritual things." Many Continental dissenting groups as well as a considerable body of Scots found new homes in the Carolinas, and by the beginning of the 18th century these people composed a majority of the population.

From France, in particular, after the revocation of the Edict of Nantes, many Huguenots who escaped from the country emigrated to South Carolina where, in spite of hardships, they apparently set an example wherever they settled.** It was an English traveler who noted that "the

* "The Fundamental Constitutions For the Carolinas," a feudal document drawn up by the philosopher John Locke and Lord Ashley, proved unsuited to the freedom-loving temper of the colonists. It was never fully applied.

** The Huguenots were to be found throughout the colonies. New Rochelle, New York, was founded by French immigrants; French clergymen were prominent in Virginia, and Paul Revere (Rivoire) of Boston was the son of a French Huguenot.

French, being a temperate and industrious people, live like one family,"[15] each assisting the others. Not infrequently, he declared, they outstripped "our English" who had more resources but managed less prudently.

The Carolina settlements were successful from the colonists' standpoint, but absentee proprietors were disappointed at lack of hoped-for profits from land sales and other enterprises, so that in 1729, proprietary interests were sold out to the Crown.

Georgia was founded by General James Charles Oglethorpe, a distinguished British soldier, Member of Parliament and man of substance, who became interested in establishing in the new world a refuge for poor debtors imprisoned under the harsh laws of the period, and other unfortunates. At the same time the British Government, alarmed at the threat to its American holdings from Spain to the south and from the French outpost in Louisiana, assumed a belated interest in supporting its American colonists. In 1732, King George II granted a charter to Oglethorpe and a group of Trustees for Georgia who were made proprietors of a tract including all the territory between the borders of South Carolina and Florida, with the customary extension "from sea to sea." Backed up by a vigorous promotional campaign in England, Oglethorpe himself led an expedition which founded a settlement at Savannah the following year.*

Georgia's charter extended religious freedom to "all persons inhabiting, or which shall inhabit or be resident within" the colony,[16] and in the next few years the Georgia settlements had gained some three thousand inhabitants. Besides Oglethorpe's British refugees, almost half of these new settlers were European Protestants—Germans, Swiss, Scots along with a few Italians and a number of Jews.

* Among those who followed Oglethorpe to America were John and Charles Wesley, the founders of Methodism, while George Whitefield, a leader of the Great Awakening, began his American ministry in Georgia.

The colony grew slowly, however. In 1752, the proprietors surrendered their rights to the Crown and Georgia, like the Carolinas, became a Royal Province.

The Spanish meanwhile had laid claim to the territory occupied by the adjacent British settlements, and in 1739 Georgia became involved in a war between the two countries. The war ended without a formal settlement of the disputed boundary. Nevertheless, the southward expansion of the British colonies had secured the Eastern seaboard between French Canada and the Spanish forts and missions in Florida.

Self-government and religious liberty were firmly established in America.

CHAPTER IV

The New England Commonwealths

That the Scriptures hold forth a perfect rule for the direction and government of all men in all duties which they are to perform to God and man. . . .

NEW HAVEN COMPACT—1639[1]

CAPTAIN John Smith, cruising off the northern American coast in 1614, gave the name "New England" to this region.[2] Much earlier, Scandinavian, Spanish, Portuguese, French, Dutch, British and possibly Irish explorers had reached these shores, but founded no permanent communities. Before the Pilgrim Fathers, extensive fishing operations were conducted on the Grand Banks, the French had set up trading posts on the St. Lawrence River, and British settlements had been established in Maine and New Hampshire.

During the decade 1630–40, over 20,000 settlers emigrated from Great Britain to Massachusetts, whence they spread throughout New England and into Nova Scotia. This exodus had its origins in the long and brilliant reign of Queen Elizabeth I, during which a movement for "purifying" the English Church arose and reached into all areas of life.

"Puritanism" was, in the broadest sense, a passion for righteousness—"the desire to know and to do God's will."*

* "Puritanism was a cutting edge which hewed liberty, democracy, humanitarianism and universal education out of the black forest of feudal Europe and the American wilderness. . . . Puritanism, therefore, is an American heritage to be grateful for."

SAMUEL ELIOT MORISON[3]

21

A basic Puritan tenet was the belief that "No man would become more honorable or wealthy than another out of any particular and singular respect to himself," but only for God's glory and the common good.[4] Such egalitarian ideals did not recommend themselves to the Stuarts. Puritans were harried by King James I and, under his son Charles I, a severe persecution broke out, in consequence of which considerable numbers migrated to America.

The Pilgrim Fathers were the wheat sifted for this planting. Not Utopia but the Bible was their guide. They were practical men with a vision, who believed that "from this little handful"[5] would arise in America a new community from which the Word of God would be a "Shining light to all the world."

The Plymouth settlement lost half its members during their first terrible winter in the new world. But when the Mayflower returned in the Spring not one of the survivors elected to sail back to England with her. America was their Promised Land.[6]

In the following months the settlers were able to plant crops and harvest them. Game was found in the forest. They celebrated their first Thanksgiving and concluded a treaty with the Indians.

Nature was not always bountiful, however, and in years of poor harvest housewives would resort to the clam banks, while some had no bread for months on end. Nevertheless, they could bear their wants cheerfully and "rest on Providence." When a serious drought threatened, the whole community had recourse to prayer, Morison relates, and were promptly rewarded by showers which revived their withered crops, to the astonishment of the local tribesmen.

Community ownership of land was superseded by a system of individual holdings, and the colony thrived.

Encouraged by the success of the Plymouth Colony, some well-to-do Puritans organized a trading corporation, The New England Council, and secured a charter from the King.

Ably led and well supplied, the Puritan immigrants established the Massachusetts Bay Colony in the Boston area.

New colonists, under the leadership of Thomas Hooker, pushed westward into the Connecticut Valley, and flourishing communities were founded in the Hartford area and at New Haven.* Dissident Puritans with Roger Williams moved into Rhode Island.** Maine, which had been settled under earlier grants, and New Hampshire, became occupied largely from Massachusetts. In a few years, Puritans had taken up much of the best land from Portland to New York.

The Puritan settlements had been founded with the aim of establishing not mere trading posts, but communities. And, while "necessity might press some (or even desire for novelty or worldly gain),"[9] it was religious conviction that drew the greater part of these multitudes to New England. Anyone comfortably situated at home would commit "a grave error," warned Governor Joseph Dudley of Massachusetts, writing in 1630, if he should come to America "for worldly ends"; but if for spiritual, he could find "what might well content him."[10]

Thus motivated, citizens of the frontier societies would create a natural school for democracy, where "the family was a little commonwealth and the commonwealth a great family."[11] John Winthrop described the character of the new commonwealth:

"That which the most in their Churches maintain as a

* Connecticut lay outside the patent of Massachusetts, and its Governor was elected by the colonists, not appointed by London. During the War for Independence, Governor Trumbull stayed in office and supported the Revolution.

** The liberal Roger Williams nevertheless shared the Puritan conviction that rights and responsibilities are two sides of the same coin. In a vivid word-picture, he compares the self-governing community to a ship where the passengers' liberties fall far short of interference with the Captain's operation of the vessel, or refusal to carry one's share of the work.[7]

"A Declaration of Rights," declared Tom Paine many years later, "is by reciprocity a Declaration of Duties also."[8]

truth in profession only, we must bring into familiar and constant practice . . . be willing to abridge ourselves of our superfluities, for the supply of others' necessities . . . make others' conditions our own—rejoice together, mourn together, labor and suffer together, and always having, before our eyes our Commission and Community in the work, our community as members of the same body, so shall we keep the unity of the spirit in the bond of peace . . . we shall find that the God of Israel is among us."[12]

New England leaders, who included an impressive number of Oxford, Cambridge and Dublin University graduates, gave a high priority to education. Harvard College was founded in 1636.* Ten years later, the Massachusetts General Court decreed that new townships of as much as 50 residents should appoint a local teacher to instruct children in reading and writing. In communities of 100 families, a "grammar school" was to be established in which pupils would be prepared to enter college.

New England townships became the first communities in the world to institute free, compulsory education. When, over 100 years afterward, Connecticut's "Western Territory" on the Great Lakes was opened to settlement, their

* Carved on the college gates is an inscription which expresses the spirit of Harvard's founders:

"After God had carried us safe to *New England*, and we had builded our houses, provided necessaries for our livelihood, reared convenient places for God's worship and settled the Civil Government; One of the next things we longed for, and looked after was to advance *Learning* and perpetuate it to Posterity dreading to leave an illiterate Ministry to the Churches, when our present Ministers shall lie in the dust."

The Charter of 1650 dedicated the college to "the advancement of all good literature, arts and sciences," and "the education of the English and Indian youth . . . in knowledge and godliness."

The first printing press in the colonies (second in the Americas) was set up in Harvard Yard in 1639.

"Ordinance" stipulated that one section of each township be reserved for the support of public schools, and the words of this Ordinance are repeated in the present Constitution of the State of Michigan.[13] New England set the educational pattern for America.

The free climate of the American colonies was no more hospitable to class distinctions than to autocratic government. When certain Puritan peers ventured a proposal to transplant the British system of hereditary nobility to the colonies, they were effectively dissuaded. For although the colonists agreed that it would be a sin against God and the magistracy to ignore the "spirit and gifts for government" with which any noble or generous family might be endowed, yet, lacking such gifts, it would be unfair to impose upon them the responsibility of high office "without sanction of divine Authority."[14] Hopes of setting up an American "aristocracy" went glimmering.

The Puritan pattern of self-government impressed itself from the beginning upon the growing settlements. As early as 1636, the Massachusetts Colony Council affirmed that "the people are not for the rulers but the rulers for the people to minister to their welfare."[15] No magistrate was to have power over the bodies or goods of the people without their consent, given as God should direct. This spirit of independence* could not fail to provoke antagonism from the British Crown, and, a few years after Boston was founded, the citizens were constrained to fortify the town,

* The popular political thinking was expressed by such writers as Samuel Danforth of Harvard, who published the following lines in 1648:

On this tree's top hangs pleasant LIBERTY.
Not seen in Austria, France, Spain, Italy.
Some fling their swords at it, their caps some cast.
In Britain 'twill not down it hangs so fast.
A looseness (true) it breeds (Galen ne'er saw)
Alas! the reason is, men eat it raw.
True liberty's there ripe, where all confess
They may do what they will, but wickedness.[16]

not against Indians or sea-roving Spaniards, but in face of an expected attack by the King's Navy. Massachusetts' first Royal Governor was imprisoned and sent back to England in custody.

Under the last of the Stuarts, an attempt was made to consolidate all the colonies north of Maryland into one "Dominion of New England." His Majesty's Government imposed a new charter upon Massachusetts severely restricting her liberties. The Rev. Increase Mather, President of Harvard College, who went to England to represent the colonists in negotiations over the charter, had to report that their demands for self-government in regard to taxes and other measures, freedom of conscience, and community control of Harvard College and the Town Meeting Houses, had all been rejected by the Committee for Trade and Foreign Plantations. A few years later Massachusetts, including Plymouth Colony and Maine, was made a Royal Province.

Further difficulties beset the colonists during the early years. Although some Indian tribes had proved friendly and numbers were converted to Christianity, two bitter conflicts, the Pequot War and "King Philip's War," had devastated the countryside.* This last struggle, in which a tenth part of Massachusetts homes were destroyed and hundreds of settlers lost their lives, was one of the most crucial in America's history.

Moreover the French, in their long warfare with England between 1690 and the Peace of Paris in 1763, enlisted the Indians in resisting the northward march of the English settlements, which suffered sporadic raids until Canada finally came under British rule.

Meanwhile, the tide of immigration continued to flow. The coastal lands filled up, and New Englanders moved into Long Island, New York and New Jersey. Nova Scotia

---

* From equatorial jungles to Arctic wastes, early Western explorers and settlers encountered native populations who, naturally, resisted the Europeans' encroachment on their territory. The Indian "problem" is by no means settled today.

had its quota of immigrants, and after 1776 British Loyalists took refuge in eastern Canada and the Bahamas. As the western territories opened up, New England farmers left their rocky fields and trekked into the Northwest Territory, across the Mississippi and the Great Plains, and over the mountains to the Pacific Coast.

New England's children peopled the land; her spirit and institutions helped shape the nation's character.

CHAPTER V

The Middle Colonies

True Godliness does not turn men out of the world, but enables them to live better in it, and excites their endeavors to mend it.

WILLIAM PENN—1669[1]

WILLIAM PENN, the founder of Pennsylvania, was the son of a British admiral. His father enjoyed the friendship of King Charles II and the Duke of York, and young Penn had been destined for a military career when he met the Quakers, more properly known as "The Society of Friends," and joined the Society.

The Quakers, who pioneered the settlement of Pennsylvania, western New Jersey and Delaware, were a liberal sect which flourished in England in the late Puritan period. Quakers practiced strict morality, believed in non-violence, and sought the "Inner Light" of God's guidance in daily life. They eschewed formal creeds, liturgy and church hierarchy, and had an antipathy to titles which, along with inherited wealth, they claimed "fill no man's head with brains or heart with truth."[2] The Quakers' egalitarian principles were reflected in their plain speech and dress.

Young Penn's family sent him to the Continent, where his acquaintance with liberal personalities and ideas was broadened by travel and study. He returned to England to become a leader in the Society and one of the most enlightened and successful colonizers in history.

The Quakers suffered persecution in England, and Penn

himself was sent to prison more than once. He became concerned with the possibility of establishing a refuge in America for the Friends, and by 1676 he had started settlements in New Jersey and appointed a commission to lay out the future city of Philadelphia.

Civil and religious liberty was to be the cornerstone of the new Quaker colony. "We lay a foundation for after ages to understand their liberty as Christians and as men," declared the Proprietors of the New Jersey colony, "that they may not be brought into bondage but by their own consent, for we put the power in the people."[3]

Immigrants from neighboring colonies settled in other sections of East and West New Jersey, which were united under a Royal Governor in 1702.

The improvident King Charles was in debt to the Penn family. In payment, he deeded over to William an enormous tract of land, which included the present States of Pennsylvania and Delaware. Penn procured a charter from the King, purchased an adjacent section of New Jersey, and fifteen years after the first Quaker immigrants, himself headed an expedition which established the colony he named "Pennsylvania" (Penn's Woods).

Dutch and Scandinavian immigrants who had preceded the Quakers lent them a hand to clear their fields and plant and harvest crops. Penn acknowledged the property rights of these neighbors, and extended to them the franchise in his colony.

No less enlightened were Penn's dealings with the local Indian tribesmen. He paid them a fair price for their lands, and strove to demonstrate that the White Man's object was "not to do them injury and thus provoke the Great Spirit, but to do good."*

English Quakers began to pour into Pennsylvania, and quickly spread throughout the colonies. They took up farms

* It was Penn's 1683 pact with the Indians to which Voltaire referred as the only one "which was never sworn to and never broken."

near Philadelphia, established trade and industry, and launched the city upon the phenomenal growth by which, in the next century, it became the metropolis of America and the second city in the British Empire. Penn himself laid out the streets of the "City of Brotherly Love," where traces of his plan can be seen today in the downtown area. The Quakers' purpose had been clearly stated by Penn and his associates. It was not "to set up factories and trade" for their own enrichment, but rather to lay "permanent foundations of temperance and virtue to support the superstructure of future happiness."[4]

"I came for the Lord's sake," Penn declared.[5]

The "permanent foundations" the Quakers were building had more to do with character than constitutions. "Good laws do well," wrote Penn in his Preface to the "Frame of Government for Pennsylvania," but "good men do better." What makes and preserves a good constitution are thus "men of wisdom and virtue" and these two attributes are naturally linked in colonial thinking. Moreover, the Quakers believed that such qualities "descend not with worldly inheritance," but must be carefully inculcated by education and example.[6]

Freedom of worship had been established by Penn and confirmed by the Pennsylvania Assembly.[7] His European travels had put him in touch with German and Swiss liberals, and many of these were attracted to Penn's "Holy Experiment" in the new world. From Germany, "Pietists" and other reformist Protestants in large numbers were led to emigrate to America* so that before long there were as many Pennsylvanians of German as English ancestry, while

* One of these pietists, a certain John Jacob Zimmerman, having enlisted 16 or 17 families, wrote in 1697 to a Quaker friend in Holland that they "designed . . . to depart from these Babylonish coasts, to those American Plantations, being led thereunto by the guidance of the Divine Spirit." Leaving their country and all their possessions that could not be carried with them, they betook themselves to Pennsylvania.[8]

31

German settlements were to be found through all the colonies from Maine to the Moravian towns of Georgia. Many an anglicized American name today can claim a German or Swiss origin.

In Northern Ireland during this period, restrictive laws oppressing the lowland Scots who had settled in Ulster provoked a massive exodus to America. Thousands emigrated to Philadelphia and out into the back country. These Ulstermen were a stalwart, God-fearing people of Calvinist background, with close-knit parochial ties. Not infrequently, an entire congregation with their pastor would remove themselves to America and settle in the same town.

Beyond the Alleghenys, new lands were settled by these late-comers as well as restless migrants from the older colonies.* The story of this western settlement is well pictured 100 years later in the diary of a Scottish traveler. Describing a party of "several families from the older settlements in the State (Pennsylvania) and from Maryland and New York to the western country," he termed them "poor enterprising people, who leave their old habitation and connections and go in quest of lands for themselves and children, with the hope of the enjoyment of independence in their worldly circumstances, where land is good and cheap." In the course of a few years, many such families began to realize their hopes, this observer noted, and the country, once a "desolate wilderness," contained many well-cultivated farms in the mountain valleys, "as far west as Pittsburgh."[9]

Upon Penn's death, his charter descended to his sons and remained in the family until the Revolution.

The first Lord Baltimore, George Calvert, was a member of an English family who settled in Ireland. Converted to Catholicism, he had hopes of establishing in Newfoundland a haven for English Catholics, then discriminated against

---

* In the west, British and French imperial interests came into conflict, and it was his achievement in saving the remnants of General Braddock's ill-fated expedition against Fort Duquesne (Pittsburgh) that brought George Washington into Colonial prominence.

in Anglican Britain. He was a member of the New England Council and the Virginia-London Company, and the success of the Virginia settlement encouraged him to obtain a contiguous grant and apply for a charter from King Charles I.

George Calvert died in 1632, and the charter was issued to his son, Cecelius. The following year, an expedition of 200 colonists was organized under the leadership of Cecelius' brother, Leonard, and a settlement was founded on Chesapeake Bay. There the Catholic colonists celebrated Mass, naming the settlement "St. Mary's" and the colony "Maryland" in honor of the Virgin Mary.*

Maryland was the first colony to prescribe religious toleration to all persons "professing to believe in Jesus Christ"[11]—a right secured by a "Statute of Toleration" passed by the first Popular Assembly in 1649. This Act proved vital to the success of the colony for, as noted by Lord Charles Baltimore a generation later, "a great part (of the first colonists) were such as could not conform . . . to the several laws of England relating to religion." Without this "general toleration," he wrote, the colony might never have been planted.[12]

The first settlers of Maryland were thus a mixed group. Although the colony had been founded by Catholic initiative, within fifty years a majority of the inhabitants were Protestants of various denominations, "those of the Church of England as well as those of the Romish faith being the fewest," Lord Baltimore had to report.[13]

The Maryland colony's progress was obstructed from the

* Wrote a Jesuit priest who accompanied the expedition, "this had never been done before in this part of the world. . . . After we had completed the sacrifice, we took upon our shoulders a great cross, which we had hewn out of a tree, and advancing in order to the appointed place, with the assistance of the Governor and his associates and the other Catholics, we erected a trophy to Christ the Saviour, humbly reciting on our bended knees the Litanies of the Sacred Cross, with great emotion."

FATHER ANDREW WHITE—1634[10]

beginning, however, by religious, political and factional strife, in addition to boundary disputes with her neighbors. The northern border was not finalized, in fact, until the surveying of the Mason and Dixon Line 100 years later.

New Netherlands was a Dutch colony founded by traders and settlers in the wake of the great explorer Henry Hudson, an Englishman in the employ of Holland. There had been little touch with this area since the brief visit of Giovanni da Verrazano in 1524, and when Henry Hudson sailed into what is now New York Bay and explored the great river that bears his name, he opened up a new region for the Hollanders' colonial ventures.

During the Netherlands' struggle with Spain, the Dutch had extended their trade and empire to the East Indies, Asia and the Americas. The Dutch East India Company was organized a year after the Pilgrims landed at Plymouth, and New Netherlands established as a Province of the Company.

Albany was founded, and Manhattan Island purchased from the Indians. Baronial estates on both sides of the river were granted under the "patroon" system, and in 1629 a "Charter of Privileges" was issued to attract settlers. The Dutch concluded a treaty with the Hartford colony defining the New York-Connecticut boundary which is still maintained today. A few years later, New Netherlands absorbed a small, neighboring settlement of Swedes and Finns.

England, apprehensive over the Dutch presence in her bailiwick, seized New Netherlands in 1664 and renamed it "New York" (in honor of the Duke of York, brother of King Charles). Ten years later, the Dutch recaptured the province, but ceded it to Britain in the peace settlement. In exchange for New York, Britain granted the Netherlanders some territory on the northern coast of South America, Dutch Guiana, where the tropical soil was considered more favorable for agricultural enterprise.

British control opened the country to further immigration from the nearby English settlements. Hither also came

German, Swiss, French, Scottish, Irish and other European émigrés, and New York began early to take on the character of a melting pot.

The sturdy Dutch settlers brought to America a robust love of liberty, for which they had engaged in a long and bitter struggle at home. For the Netherlanders, as for the British, freedom was the child of faith, and both were nourished by education. Their Charter included a stipulation that the colony "support a minister and a schoolmaster so that the service of God and zeal for religion may not grow cool among us."

The same resolve was expressed in the next century by the founders of King's College (later, Columbia University) in a public prospectus. The aim of the College was "not to impose upon the scholars, the peculiar tenets of any particular sect of Christians," but to inculcate "the great principles of Christianity and morality in which true Christians of every denomination are generally agreed." After enumerating courses covering a broad field of studies, this statement concluded: "and finally to lead the students from a study of nature to a knowledge of themselves and of the God of nature, and their duty to Him, themselves and one another and everything that can contribute to their true happiness both here and hereafter."[14]

In New York was held the landmark trial of John Peter Zenger, proprietor of the New York Weekly Journal, who was prosecuted for printing "seditious libel" against the government. Ably defended by Andrew Hamilton, a prominent Philadelphia lawyer, Zenger was acquitted, and freedom of the press thus established in America as early as 1735.

The first New York State Constitution secured the rule of civil and religious liberty, "as required by the benevolent principles of national liberty."

At the time of the Revolution, Britain's American colonies numbered thirteen—in effect thirteen separate commonwealths. Out of the rich diversity of their people unity was not easily born. Nevertheless, above divisions rose a common hope. To Puritan and Cavalier, black-hatted Quaker and black-frocked Jesuit, America held out the promise of a future in which all men could walk together as children of God. This vision, the driving force of America's history, remains today America's hope.

VIRTUE

CHAPTER VI

The Great Awakening

I doubt if there is any problem—social, political or economic—that will not melt before the fire of a spiritual awakening.

FRANKLIN D. ROOSEVELT[1]

THE frontier developed courage, initiative and responsibility. However, dangers, hardships and endless physical toil took their toll of the American frontiersmen. Indian wars in the New England colonies exhausted the people. In the thriving seacoast cities, on the other hand, prosperity tended to soften the moral fibre of the citizens. A debasement of character and culture began to mark the second and third generation of settlers.*

Colonial leaders took measures to counteract this decline in standards. In 1715, a Resolution of the Colonial Assembly of Connecticut deplored the fact that "the glory has departed from us," and urged an inquiry into the causes and possible cure of this degeneracy. After the close of the war with the Narraganset Indians, the Assembly appointed a day of "solemn fasting and prayer," and recommended that ministers throughout the colony instruct the people in religious duties and awaken them to "repentance and a

---

* "In New England the once raging fires of Puritanism were banked. People in general attended 'meeting', . . . kept holy (outwardly, at least) the Sabbath, and attempted to observe the other commandments, but they were falling away from the antique faith."

SAMUEL ELIOT MORISON[2]

general reformation of manners." Similar steps were advo-
cated by the Legislature the following spring.[3]

"The Great Awakening" was a moral and spiritual revival, the first colony-wide movement in America, which had
its beginnings in New Jersey with the Rev. Theodorus
Freylinghuysen, a Dutch Reformed clergyman of German
ancestry. Starting in 1726, the influence of his preaching
soon spread into Pennsylvania and New York. At about this
time, in Philadelphia, William Tennant, a Scotch-Irish
immigrant, founded a school with the aim of training young
men for the ministry. "The Log College of Neshaminy," as
it was called, removed to Princeton, where it was hoped to
establish in the middle colonies an institution of higher
learning to rank with Harvard, Yale and William and
Mary. "The College of New Jersey" (later, Princeton University), which grew out of these initiatives, provided much
of the leadership of the Awakening in the middle and
southern colonies.

Jonathan Edwards, the leader of The Great Awakening
in New England, was the greatest intellect produced by
colonial America. While hardly in his teens, Edwards had
written precocious essays. He was converted at the age of
seventeen during his senior year at Yale, where he graduated
at the head of his class.* He made original observations in
the fields of electricity and sound, and was one of the first
to introduce America to Newton's physics and the philosophy of Locke. Edwards might have become a great scientist
or literary figure, but his passion was theology—the study
of God's relation to the world and to Man.

* Another of Yale's contributions to the Movement was David Brainard, "the Apostle to the Indians." Converted when an undergraduate,
Brainard committed his life and ministry to the aboriginal tribes and,
although early stricken with an incurable disease, he continued his
ministry, which took him as far as New York and Pennsylvania.
Brainard's "Journal" was published in many editions, and his influence on the youth of the colonies, as well as the Indians, was far-
reaching.

Many things can change a man's attitudes and actions, Edwards preached, but only the Power of a Creator can change his nature or "give him a new nature."[4] Moving out from his pastorate at Northampton, Edwards preached to congregations throughout Massachusetts and Connecticut, where his influence was profound and permanent. It was astonishing, Edwards wrote, to see the transformation in certain towns where the people, formerly vain or vicious, had "gone over to a new world." Old grudges were wiped out, friendships renewed, enemies reconciled, these changes "abiding on multitudes all over the land for a year and a half."[5]

Jonathan Edwards remained withal a humble Christian, gratefully aware of his need for "more wisdom" than he possessed. It was his rule "to lay hold on light" and embrace it, "although held forth by a child or an enemy."[6]

The Great Awakening shook New England. Edwards' published sermons, and books in which he described miracles of spiritual rebirth in individuals and whole communities, were read throughout the colonies and across the seas.*

In far-away Georgia, George Whitefield read of Edwards' work as he was starting his own career as a revivalist. Traveling up and down the land, Whitefield gave his message in hundreds of assemblages, where people came from miles around to hear him, adding impetus to the Awakening across the whole country. He had a powerful voice, and could be heard by as many as twenty thousand people, who

* Edwards recorded the revival in the Connecticut Valley in a pamphlet entitled "A Faithful Narrative of the Surprising Work of God in the Conversion of Many Hundred Souls in Northampton." John Wesley read this work in England; "Surely this is the Lord's doing," he wrote in his Journal, "and marvelous in our eyes."

Benjamin Franklin urged his sister to read one of Edwards' sermons.

In 1757, Jonathan Edwards was elected President of the College of New Jersey, but died before he could take office.

would stand during his open-air meetings when the largest halls could not contain the crowds.

Whitefield kindled a flame of faith in communities from Georgia to Maine. In Charleston, people shut up their shops, forgot their business and "laid aside their schemes for this world." The more often he preached, the more they desired to hear him again.* "Eternal themes, the tremendous solemnities of our religion, were all alive upon his tongue."[8]

In Massachusetts, Whitefield preached to crowds of seven thousand in Cambridge; to fifteen thousand on Boston Common.[9] Benjamin Franklin remarked upon the multitudes who came to listen to his sermons in Philadelphia, and recounted the wonderful change that soon became apparent, "in half our inhabitants." From being thoughtless or indifferent toward religion, Franklin reported, "all the world was growing religious . . . so that one could not walk through the town of an evening without hearing psalms sung by families in every street."[10]

Such manifestations were not welcomed, however, in every quarter. The work of God which had been so remarkably begun in New England would encounter pharisaical animosity from "some that profess the greatest regard to religion."[11] Jonathan Edwards was forced to leave his church in Northampton. Benjamin Trumbull, the Connecticut historian, refers to "unreasonable and powerful opposition" in Hebron as well as "clamors about errors and disorders" which attended the movement in that town. Trumbull, who was a native of the community, nevertheless records the permanent effects for good produced there by "the most glorious and extensive revival of religion and reformation of manners which this country ever experienced."[12]

* A ship-builder who had been prejudiced against Whitefield was persuaded to go to a meeting. Asked what he thought of the preacher afterwards, he replied: "Think! I never heard such a man in my life! I tell you, every Sunday when I go to Church, I can build a ship from stem to stern under the sermon; but, were it to save my soul, under Mr. Whitefield, I could not lay a single plank!"[7]

The influence of the Great Awakening reached into every sphere of colonial life. Of the nine colleges established in the colonies before the Revolution, six had their origins in this period.* In the four southern colonies, where the Anglican Church had at first remained lukewarm toward Whitefield, the revival sparked a change of religious affiliation. As a result, by the time of the Revolution, church membership had become overwhelmingly Baptist, Presbyterian and Methodist, which it remains today. Recent studies in Virginia and Connecticut have confirmed that, between the years 1763–1776, support for the approaching Revolution was most active in areas where the Awakening had made its strongest impact.**

In Virginia, a far-reaching social revolution took place in the decade 1770–80. Repeal of the laws of entail and primogeniture tended to break up the great land-holdings; the Statute for Religious Freedom, passed in 1786, promoted tolerance; the spread of education and extension of the franchise put more power into the hands of the people. "Undoubtedly, the Great Awakening was one of the contributing factors to the development of democracy in Virginia," states Wesley Gewehr. "The very nature of the evangelical movement and its teachings worked for democracy." Many forces contributed, he concludes, toward this revolution in the Old Dominion, but "one cannot say that the least of these was the rise of evangelical Christianity and the development of the popular churches."[14]

* Harvard College was founded in 1636; William and Mary in 1693; Yale in 1701; The College of New Jersey (later Princeton), 1746; Franklin's Academy, founded in 1751, became the University of Pennsylvania; King's College, eventually Columbia University, was founded in 1754; Rhode Island College, founded in 1764, was renamed Brown University in 1804; Queen's College, 1766, became Rutgers University; Dartmouth College was founded in 1769.

** "Calvinism, and Edwards, provided pre-Revolutionary America with a radical, even democratic, social and political ideology, and evangelical religion embodied, and inspired, a thrust toward American nationalism."

ALAN HEIMERT[13]

The Great Awakening rallied America's spiritual forces at the dawn of her independence. "Religion, always a principle of energy in this new people," noted Edmund Burke in 1775, "is also one main cause of this free spirit." And the expanding revival movement insured that Christianity would move forward with the frontier.* The new American, like his colonial forefathers, would inherit a Christian tradition.**

* "The American tradition—of Populists and rank and file Jacksonians and Jeffersonians—was hardly the child of the Age of Reason. It was born of the 'New Light' imparted to the American mind by the Awakening and the evangelical clergy of colonial America."

ALAN HEIMERT[15]

** Writing in 1835, the French observer Alexis de Tocqueville would comment that religion, while it had no establishment here, "exerted more influence in America than in any other country."[16]

JOIN, or DIE.

CHAPTER VII

The Colonies Come of Age

RESOLVED:—that there are certain essential rights . . .
which are founded in the law of God and nature, and
are the common rights of all mankind.

MASSACHUSETTS HOUSE OF REPRESENTATIVES
—October 29, 1765

THE Great Awakening took place 125 years after the first
settlements had been planted. The colonies had grown
and prospered, with their metropolis, Philadelphia, second
only to London in the British Empire. The general standard
of living was higher in America than in the mother country.
The colonies boasted over 3,000 churches and eight colleges.
Schools were widespread and newspapers and periodicals
circulated freely.

America produced a galaxy of outstanding leaders during
this period. George Washington was born in 1732; John
Adams in 1735; Thomas Jefferson in 1743; James Madison
in 1751; Alexander Hamilton in 1755. Samuel Adams was
born in 1722 and Benjamin Franklin, one of the oldest of
the Founders, in 1706. Such men proved capable of grasping
a revolutionary situation, shaping a nation's character and
directing its destiny.*

Colonial America had no central government, each col-

---

* "I know of only three times in the western world when statesmen
consciously took control of historic destinies: Periclean Athens, Rome
under Augustus, and the founding of your American republic."

ALFRED NORTH WHITEHEAD[1]

ony being administered under the authority of a Governor and Council, with a popular Assembly elected by the citizens. In most of the colonies, the Governor was appointed by the Crown, and clashes not infrequently occurred between the provincial Assemblies and their Royal Governors. Armed uprisings took place in Virginia, Maryland, North Carolina and New York; Connecticut's charter once had to be hidden in the "Charter Oak" to escape confiscation by the Crown and, in Massachusetts, Governor Edmund Andros was clapped into prison by the townspeople of Boston.

This struggle for self-government fostered a national spirit in America, and many forces contributed to it. The Great Awakening exerted, as we have seen, a colony-wide influence, while the growth of cultural and educational institutions, the circulation of periodicals, and an expanded postal service encouraged communications between the different sections of the country.

Moreover, the fight for survival against hostile savages had, from the beginning, drawn the settlements together. During the French and Indian War, a united strategy was attempted by the colonies in a Congress at Albany, New York.*

By 1765, the Stamp Act and other British encroachments on colonial rights had stirred national opposition. In the provincial towns, secret organizations calling themselves "Sons of Liberty" were formed. Adopting direct action by meetings and demonstrations, they aroused the people to the issues on which the approaching war for independence would be fought.

The Stamp Act Congress, drawing representatives from nine colonies, met in New York and passed resolutions protesting to the British Government against the offensive measures.

* The "Albany Plan" was drafted by Benjamin Franklin. It suffered "the singular fate," as he recorded, of being repudiated by the colonial Assemblies on the ground of excessive "prerogative," while the London Government rejected it as having "too much of the democratic."[2]

As American opposition to British policies hardened, "Committees of Correspondence" were organized throughout the colonies. These were cells of patriots who kept in touch with each other by courier (Paul Revere was one of them), and became nerve-centers of the growing resistance movement—"the happiest means of cementing the union and acting in concert,"[3] as John Adams expressed it.

Colonial resistance was brought to a boil by a British tax imposed upon tea. Patriots boycotted the beverage; tea ships were prevented from unloading their cargoes. On the night of November 28, 1773, a band of "Sons of Liberty," disguised as Indians, boarded three British vessels, overpowered the crews, and dumped 342 chests of tea into Boston Harbor.* British counter-measures resulted in

*A NEW SONG

As near beauteous Boston lying
On the gently swelling flood
Without jack or pennant flying,
Three ill-fated tea ships rode.

Just as glorious Sol was setting,
On the Wharf, a numerous crew,
Sons of freedom, fear forgetting,
Suddenly appeared in view.

Armed with hammers, axe and chisels,
Weapons for warlike deed,
Towards the herbage-freighted vessels,
They approached with dreadful speed.

Quick as thought the ships were boarded
Hatches burst and chests displayed;
Axes, hammers help afforded;
What a glorious crash they made.

Squash into the deep descended,
Cursed weed of China's coast;
Thus at once our fears were ended;
British rights shall ne'er be lost.

Captains! Once more hoist your streamers
Spread your sails and plough the wave;

stiffening American resistance. The confrontation, which had originated in the colonists' protest against violation of their rights as British citizens, would finally effect the separation of her colonies from the mother country.

Democratic ideas, brought to the colonies with the first settlers, found a congenial climate in the new world. John Wise of Ipswich, a leader in the opposition to Governor Andros, had stated as a "fundamental principle relating to government" that under God "all power is originally in the people," and described Democracy in church and state as "a very honorable and regular government according to the dictates of right reason."* And by 1762, James Otis was basing his argument for colonial rights on the "general proposition (that) God made all men naturally equal."[4]

In New England, Election Days had provided a platform for some prominent clergymen to make an Address to the Governor and Colonial Assembly. On these occasions, Puritan preachers would harp on provocative themes, such as "The Character of a Good Ruler,"[5] and "On the Power and Limitation of Magistrates."[6] The Rev. John Bulkley of New Haven, for example, concluded such a discourse by asserting, "No law of civil magistrate can bind in opposition to the Divine . . . all must be done in subordination to those laws of God."[7] These invocations were published and circulated throughout the land.

Meanwhile, the youth of the colonies were being educated in the philosophy of human rights and responsibilities. Twenty years before the Revolution, Francis Alison in the College of Philadelphia was teaching his students that "every right is divine that is constituted by the law

Tell your masters they were dreamers,
When they thought to cheat the brave.

"The Boston Tea Party" inspired the above ballad, which appeared in the "Pennsylvania Gazette" December, 1773.

* Wise's *Vindication of the Government of New England Churches* (1717) was republished in 1772 and widely read.

of God and nature," with the corollary that "princes were constituted for the good of the people."[8] President John Witherspoon* of the College of New Jersey and George Wythe of William and Mary College, Thomas Jefferson's teacher, were imparting identical truths to the nation's future leaders. In New York, a King's College student publicly defended the Colonies' demands against an attack by a future Episcopal Bishop.** "The sacred rights of mankind were written by the hand of Divinity itself," wrote 19-year-old Alexander Hamilton, "and can never be erased or obscured by mortal power."[9]

The American revolutionaries, like Cromwell's Covenanters before them, "knew what they were fighting for and loved what they knew."[10] The writings of the Adamses, Jefferson and John Dickinson were well known. As the final break with Britain drew near, a flood of letters, essays and articles in the press created a public opinion increasingly concerned with "natural rights" and determined to preserve them.†

At the beginning of the war, Tom Paine's "Common Sense" swept the country, reaching a readership extensive even by present standards.

The Declaration of Independence had been preceded by such colonial proclamations as the Virginia Bill of Rights,

* Witherspoon preached a sermon at Princeton, May 17, 1776, being the general fast appointed by the Congress. In this discourse, which bore the impressive title, "The Dominion of God over the Passions of Men," he stated his reasons for concurring in the Americans' demand for control of their own affairs.

** The Rev. Samuel Seabury, later first Bishop of the Protestant Episcopal Church in the United States, wrote in 1774 under the name of "A. W. Farmer" (A Westchester Farmer) supporting the Loyalist position.

† "In establishing American independence, the pen and the press had merit equal to that of the sword . . . the exertions of the army would have been insufficient to effect the revolution unless the great body of the people had been prepared for it and also kept in a constant disposition to oppose Great Britain."

DAVID RAMSAY—1789[11]

the Mecklenburg County (North Carolina) Resolutions, and the Suffolk Resolves (carried posthaste from Boston to the Congress in Philadelphia by Paul Revere).

Acts of legislatures must conform to natural right and justice, summed up George Mason, author of the Virginia Declaration. The laws of nature are the laws of God, the Supreme Authority over every earthly power:

"The Legislature must not obstruct our obedience to Him from Whose punishments they cannot protect us," concluded Mason. "All human constitutions which contradict (His) laws, we are in conscience bound to disobey."[12]

In professing "a decent respect to the opinions of mankind,"[13] moreover, Americans would be submitting their case to the court of world opinion. In Britain itself, although speeches in Parliament by former Prime Minister William Pitt (Lord Chatham) and Edmund Burke supporting America* failed to sway the Government, a press campaign masterminded by John Adams and Ben Franklin had won over an important section of the public to the American cause. In France, forthcoming aid for the embattled Americans would be assured by the popularity of "Bonhomme Richard" no less than by Franklin's diplomacy.**

Soon the world would hear about certain truths assumed by the former colonists to be self-evident: equality of all men under God; unalienable rights which it was the function of governments to secure; governments, moreover,

* "When your Lordships consider their decency, firmness and wisdom, you cannot but respect their cause and wish to make it your own," Chatham told the House of Lords, "for solidity of reasoning, force of sagacity and wisdom of conclusion . . . no body of men can stand in preference to the general Congress of Philadelphia . . . and all attempts to impose servitude upon such a mighty continental nation must be vain."

** The popular philosophy of Franklin's "Poor Richard's Almanack" had been published in France under the title, "Le Science de Bonhomme Richard."

48

whose powers would be derived from the consent of the governed; and, finally, the fateful proposition:

> "That whenever any form of government becomes destructive of these ends
> It is the right of the people to alter or abolish it,
> And to institute new government,
> Laying its foundations on such principles and organizing its powers in such form,
> As to them shall seem most likely to effect their safety and happiness."[14]

CHAPTER VIII

The Faith That Built America

The foundation of every government is some principle
or passion in the mind of the people.

JOHN ADAMS—1776[1]

THE political philosophy of America's Founders stemmed
from their acceptance of a universal moral law—a law
which they believed to be the expression of God's authority
in the affairs of men. "Before any human institutions of
government were known in the world," wrote Tom Paine,
"there existed a compact between God and man."[2] This
credo was affirmed by Patrick Henry speaking out against
the appeasers of his day,[3] no less than by John Adams, who
rallied the waverers in Congress with the assurance that
"There's a Divinity that shapes our ends!"[4]

During the war, a considerable section of the population
had been indifferent—even opposed—to independence.*
Yet the American Revolution was attended by few of the
bloody excesses usual in such conflicts, nor had it been concluded, like so many others, by "a subversion of the liberty
it was intended to establish."[6]

Half a century afterwards, Abraham Lincoln would pose
the question: What great principle held the Confederation
together? It was, he judged, "that sentiment in the Declara-

* "As to the people, in the early periods of the war, near one half
of them were avowedly more attached to Great Britain than to their
liberty."

ALEXANDER HAMILTON—1782[5]

tion of Independence that gave liberty not alone to the people of this country, but hope to all the world for all future time."[7]

Liberty, like life itself, is the gift of God,[8] Thomas Jefferson believed, and it was in this "sentiment" that the Founders committed lives, fortunes and sacred honor to their revolutionary venture in nation-building.

With the news of Yorktown, the first act of the Congress was to adjourn, march in a body to a nearby church, and there offer thanks to Heaven for the victory of American arms.*

Victory, however, brought further challenges. The Articles of Confederation under which the former colonists had with difficulty managed to conduct the war proved even less adequate to the demands of peace. The new States quarrelled and quickly became divided over local issues. These divisions were reflected in the Convention which met in Philadelphia during the summer of 1787 to revise the Articles or, as it turned out, to draft a Constitution for the new Republic.

"The noble struggle" which they had made in the cause of liberty had indeed occasioned, as Alexander Hamilton declared, "a kind of revolution in human sentiment."[10] The delegates were conscious that the eyes of the world were upon them. Nevertheless, prospects for agreement often appeared hopeless, and even Washington, presiding over the four months of sessions, complained that "we are one nation today and thirteen tomorrow!"[11]

In the "Miracle at Philadelphia" James Madison could not fail to perceive the finger of Divine intervention.[12] The Charter which was born out of the deliberations of the

* Governor Jonathan Trumbull was following a current practice when he reminded the Connecticut legislators of their forefathers' example, and exhorted them to invoke Divine guidance in their councils.[9] During the war, as Franklin later reminded the Constitutional Convention, the Congress had designated special days of "Fasting, humiliation and prayer," and this tradition is still maintained in the United States Congress' custom of opening its sessions with prayer.

Convention "ranks above every written Constitution"[13] and has provided a model and inspiration for governments around the world.

To create a national government out of the thirteen emergent States, a new public opinion had to be aroused and mobilized. Decisive in the ratification of the Constitution by the people was *The Federalist*—a series of 85 articles written by James Madison, Alexander Hamilton and John Jay, respectively future President, Secretary of the Treasury and Chief Justice of the Supreme Court of the United States. Termed by Jefferson "the best commentary on the principles of government ever written,"[14] these pieces were published in the newspapers and widely read and studied.

The theme of *The Federalist* was national unity. "The prosperity of the people depends upon their remaining firmly united," wrote Jay early in this series. During the war, the strength of the revolutionists had lain not in their numbers but in their unity, and with the Founders, union was ever "the most sacred thing."[15] To the Continental Congress, Patrick Henry had proclaimed, "I am not a Virginian but an American!" The Declaration of Independence itself was the product of a team—Jefferson, Adams, Franklin, Livingston and Sherman—with an overall review by Congress.*

Jefferson himself believed that the last hope of liberty in the world rested on the United States, and "for so dear a state"[16] he was ready to sacrifice every personal interest. "We are all Republicans, we are all Federalists!" he would declare after a bitter Presidential campaign. John Adams struck the same note[17] and George Washington, whose abhorrence of "the spirit of party" was proverbial, laid emphasis in his "Farewell Address" upon the need of the American people to preserve and cherish their national unity.

In establishing a republican government and vesting

* "We must all hang together," quipped Franklin to John Hancock, "or we shall most assuredly hang separately."

power in the people, the Founders were making a radical experiment. Kindred attempts, "formed with the seeds of their own dissolution" had failed in the past. It was essential that this political building be set upon sure foundations.

The Founders entertained few illusions about human nature.* They feared the tyranny of the mob no less than that of a monarch.** Dedication to self-government was based, nevertheless, on faith in the people's capacity to support it. John Adams, though mistrustful of democratic "excesses," acknowledged that the people not infrequently saw further than he did on fundamental issues.[18] Alexander Hamilton, no advocate of a classless society, believed that "the fabric of American empire" must rest on the solid basis of "Consent of the Governed." The stream of national power, he wrote, "ought to flow immediately from that pure, original fountain of all legitimate authority."[19]

Power, it was recognized, must be delegated to rulers, but it ought frequently to revert to the people, who were "its only safe depositories."[20] It was to this end that annual elections were favored by some,[21] and even "a little rebellion" might be tolerated as a "medicine necessary for the sound health of government."[22]

In the Founders' philosophy of government, democratic ideas were linked with deeper currents of thought and feeling. A republican government is best, John Adams was convinced, "in a certain state of society," and in America "the morals of the people not only bear it but require it."[23] Public virtue is the true basis of republican government, he believed, and by "virtue" he clearly meant more than

* "The American Government and Constitution (are) the work of men who believed in original sin," wrote James Bryce in explaining the principle of separation of powers, "and were resolved to leave open for transgressors no door which they could possibly shut."

** "Well, what have we got, Doctor, a republic or a monarchy?" asked a woman in the crowd outside Constitution Hall in Philadelphia as the delegates emerged. "A Republic—if you can keep it," replied Franklin.

mere conformity to legal codes or social mores. "There must be a positive passion for the public good,"[24] Adams declared. That "republics live by virtue"[25] was an axiom with the Founders. A republic without virtue would be "an absurdity in politics"[26] which could no more stand than a building when the foundation is removed. And liberty itself, apart from morality, could be "nothing but an empty sound"[27]—a "Body without a soul"[28] which might continue to exist in form but would be lost in essence.[29] Where virtue is its object, on the contrary, "a Commonwealth flourishes"[30] secure in the "armour" which renders it invincible against its foes.[31]

In his Farewell Address, George Washington saw religion and morality as indispensable supports for political prosperity, and above all a "necessary spring" for popular government. To him it was unthinkable that the permanent felicity of a people was not connected by Providence with its virtue. Further, Washington was quick to caution the American people against the delusion that "morality can be maintained apart from religious principle."*

Moral fibre was judged to be so essential an element in the democratic process that the United States Senate took the occasion of President Washington's First Inaugural to assure him of their conviction that national policy must be based upon private morality. "For the hope of public virtue must be frustrated," they concluded, "if individuals be not influenced by moral principle."**

American statesmen found themselves unequivocally in

* Washington, like the Pilgrim Fathers before him, compared the founding of America with the establishment of Israel in the Promised Land, "by the same wonder-working Deity."[32] Succeeding Presidents have followed Washington's example in acknowledging publicly the nation's dependence upon Divine favor.

** 100 years before the Constitution, William Penn pictured this principle in a simile where he compared the course of government with a clock. Both go, he explained, "from the motion men give them." Good men will produce good government or, if bad, they will change it. "But bad men will demoralise the best government."[33]

55

support of separation between Church and State ("a loathesome combination" in Jefferson's view).[34] Yet, more than wealth or armaments, wise and good men constituted to them the strength of a state and it followed that nothing could be of more importance than "to form and train up youth in wisdom and virtue."[35] It must be the responsibility of Government to nurture these qualities,[36] and the Massachusetts Constitution stipulated that along with wisdom and knowledge the promotion of virtue was to be an unmistakable aim of public instruction. "The fear and love of Deity," it was assumed, must be inculcated in the minds of youth, as well as the principles of morality so essential to the preservation of our liberties.[37]

Thomas Jefferson himself had no doubt that the Creator had subjected mankind to "the moral law of his nature."[38] Moral imperatives were "not to be effaced by the subtleties of our brain,"[39] and it was under Jefferson's leadership that the University of Virginia was striving to develop a rounded education—moral, political and economic—the advantages of which would truly be "beyond all estimate."[40]*

The idea of establishing inherent rights of the individual and building a nation upon them is, fundamentally, not of political but of religious origin. It sprang out of the Reformation and its struggles. It was nourished by the Scriptures, and matured in the long history of the Christian Church.

The men who secured our liberties took their conception of man from this tradition. They were heirs of a common faith, reared in the belief that the true foundation of government is "the unchangeable will of God."[42] The whole structure of society was built upon men's relationship with their Creator, and the right to nationhood itself was confirmed by natural and divine law.

This faith inspired the Founders' hopes, sustained them

* The province of the Professor of Ethics would embrace "proof of the existence of God . . . and the laws and obligations which these inferred."[41]

through difficulties and dangers, and pointed to a common destiny for mankind.

Writing in his old age to his grandson, George Washington Adams, John Adams defined the whole duty of man as "obedience to God's will."[43] In this, he was expressing a life-long conviction. "From a sense of the government of God should all our actions originate," he had recorded in his diary half a century before, "and this master-passion in a good man's soul will swallow up and destroy all the rest."[44]

In this article of faith, John Adams perfectly interpreted the ideology which mastered the Founders of the American Republic.

CHAPTER IX

George Washington

The simple truth is
his greatest eulogy.*
ABIGAIL ADAMS[1]

GEORGE Washington was born in 1732 on his family's plantation in Westmoreland County in Virginia. His great-grandfather had emigrated from Yorkshire, England, and the Washingtons had been substantial people in the colony—planters, magistrates and Members of the House of Burgesses.

When George was eleven years old, his father died and he was left under the guardianship of his mother and the guidance of two older half-brothers. As was not uncommon in those days, many of the copy-book sentences from which he learned to read and write consisted of moral precepts. His copy book can be seen today in the Library of Congress in Washington. Its last line reads:

"Labor to keep alive in your heart that little spark of celestial fire called conscience."

Attending the local school, young George excelled in

* "For his was the singular destiny and merit, of leading the armies of his country successfully through an arduous war, for the establishment of its independence; of conducting its councils through the birth of a government, new in its forms and principles . . . and scrupulously obeying the laws through the whole of his career, civil and military, of which the history of the world furnishes no other example."
THOMAS JEFFERSON—1814[2]

sports and horsemanship. He applied himself to his lessons and read the books in his brother's library. He developed an interest in mathematics and, by the age of fourteen, had gained a practical knowledge of surveying.

Young Washington was six feet tall and powerfully built. While still in his teens, he had thoughts of going to sea, following the example of his half-brother Lawrence. His mother opposed the idea, however, and a year later he accepted a job with a surveying expedition offered him by Lord Fairfax, the Proprietor of the Colony, who was a cousin of Lawrence's wife. Soon George was appointed surveyor for Fairfax County. In the next three years, his work took him into the western country beyond the Alleghenys, where he acquired the extensive knowledge of the frontier which would prove valuable in his future career.

It was by the thorough performance of commonplace daily duties that George Washington was building slowly "that stronger structure of the spirit that men call character," through which he would live and grow to fit "the elaborate cloak of praise" to be fashioned for him.[3] At the age of 20, he had been appointed adjutant of one of Virginia's four military districts, and the following year, with the French and Indian War impending, Governor Dinwiddie sent him on a mission into the Ohio Valley to deliver a warning to the encroaching French. It was here that Washington commanded the first, and unsuccessful, expedition against Fort Duquesne, a French outpost. Shortly thereafter he resigned his commission in protest against British discrimination in regard to colonial officers.

A year later, he was appointed a special aide to the British General Braddock in the campaign against the French and their Indian allies. In their first engagement, Braddock ignored young Colonel Washington's warning about the guerrilla tactics of the natives; the British regulars marched into an ambush, and were massacred. Washington managed to organize a retreat of the survivors, including the dying Braddock. He spent 24 hours in the saddle, had two horses shot under him and received four bullets through his coat. His heroic action during this disastrous encounter added to the respect in which Washington was held throughout Virginia.*

During the remainder of the war, Washington served as Commander-in-Chief of the Virginia forces, and maintained a line of forts on the frontier. In 1758, he joined the expedition which raised the British flag again over Fort Duquesne (renamed Fort Pitt), and saw the abandonment of French hopes for an American Empire.**

Washington then resigned his commission as a Colonial Officer. He was elected to the Virginia House of Burgesses, in which he served until he was sent to Philadelphia as a Delegate to the First Continental Congress. About this time, he met and fell in love with a young widow, Martha Dandridge Custis, who had two small children and a large property. The following year they were married. She remained throughout his life a devoted and capable partner, while he was a loving husband, and a true father to his stepchildren.

By the time of the Revolution, George Washington was counted as a wealthy man. Land-owner, farmer, respected public official, he could have much to lose through revolution. Moreover, he was a Vestryman in the Established

* In 1755, after General Braddock's disaster, the Rev. Samuel Davies, a leader of the Awakening in Virginia, concluded a militant sermon with a prophetic tribute to "that heroic youth, Colonel George Washington whom . . . Providence has hitherto preserved in so signal a manner for some important service to his country."[4]

** An incident revealing of Washington's character took place during this period. A dispute arose between him and a Mr. Payne, and hot words passed. They separated and Washington got a grip on his temper. Next day, he met Payne and apologized, frankly admitting he had been at fault.

He later wrote of himself, "It is with pleasure that I receive reproof when reproof is due because no man can be readier to accuse me than I am to acknowledge error when I am guilty of one, nor more desirous of atoning for a crime when I am guilty of one."[5]

Church and had been an officer in the British Army. Like most colonials, his family roots were deep in England.

During his fifteen years in the House of Burgesses, however, Washington had followed closely the development of the Colonies' breach with the mother-country. He was stirred by Patrick Henry's oratory, and took a hand, with George Mason and Thomas Jefferson, in the passage of the Virginia Resolves; he supported the denunciations of the Stamp Act and joined in the call for a General Congress of the American Colonies to take action against British encroachments upon American liberties.

In 1770, Washington made a third visit to the western Pennsylvania country, with which he was now familiar. Here the authority of Britain had been established over an immense territory, and he must have pondered over the future relations of this potential empire with the government in far-away London.

Events were now moving inexorably toward an eventual break between America and Britain. After the tax on tea was levied, Washington joined in a colony-wide boycott, and banned the beverage from his estates. When armed resistance appeared imminent as a result of the closing of the Port of Boston, Washington was ready to raise 1000 men, "subsist them" at his own expense, and march at their head to the support of the embattled New Englanders.[6]

At the First Continental Congress in Philadelphia, Washington, although he possessed neither the forensic powers of Patrick Henry nor Jefferson's facility of expression, was recognized for knowledge of facts and sound judgment as "unquestionably the greatest man on the floor."[7]

For in George Washington was found that quality of the leader, a "manifest dependability," which his great biographer Douglas Southall Freeman attributes to his early but deliberate decision to adhere to what he termed "the principles which govern my conduct."[8] These principles were adopted by him and applied habitually and earnestly in his contact with the hard realities of military life on the frontier. "Old, old principles they were, but principles disdained in every generation by so many that their rediscovery is a thrill and their application an adventure; young Washington resolved to adhere resolutely to truth, to practice rigid honesty, to do his full duty, to put forth his largest effort, to maintain uniform courtesy and, above all, to deal justly."[9]

By May 10, 1775, when the Second Continental Congress met in Philadelphia, Paul Revere had spread the alarm and war had already begun at Lexington and Concord. George Washington had firmly decided to devote his "life and fortune to this cause."[10] He made an impression upon his fellow Delegates when he took his seat in the Congress wearing the buff-and-blue uniform of his Fairfax County militia.[11] Nominated, on John Adams' suggestion, as Commander-in-Chief of the Continental forces, he was unanimously elected by the Congress.

George Washington's military experience had been acquired in militia operations and Indian fighting on the frontier, and his political career limited to the Virginia House of Burgesses. Nevertheless, he succeeded throughout the war in holding the country and the army together when often there seemed to be neither unity nor hope of victory. Serving without pay himself, he trained his "Ragged Continentals" and built them into an effective fighting force. He labored to unite the divided and demoralized Congress in support of his troops, and expended much time and patient effort in correspondence with Congressional Committees and State governing bodies. "When the States were falling apart," concludes Freeman, "he was the moral cement of the union."[12]

Washington had been given a task beyond human strength. The fact that he was able to fulfill it is clear evidence of a religious faith which was "yoked with devotion, pride and patience in carrying him through the dark morass of disappointment and defeat." It was not creedal religion, "but faith born out of his own experience, 'Providence having so often taken us up when bereft of every other hope.' "[13]

Although a strict disciplinarian, Washington was idolized by his men, because in him they could see exemplified the cause for which America had taken up arms.*

The general built a staff of outstanding young officers, like "Light Horse Harry" Lee, Alexander Hamilton, and the Marquis of Lafayette, then only twenty years old. "The father of his country" was a father to these young men whose lives were profoundly influenced by his example.

With Cornwallis' surrender at Yorktown, America's independence was secured. After the treaty of peace with Britain was finally signed, Washington resigned his commission and retired once more to Mount Vernon.**

Freedom from British rule was, to be sure, only the first step in establishing a viable nation. Disputes over trade and other matters severely strained relations between the former colonies. Conferences at Alexandria (in which Washington took an unofficial but key part)[16] and Annapolis prepared the ground for a Convention to be held in Philadelphia during the summer of 1787.

The stated purpose of the Philadelphia Convention was "to revise the Articles of Confederation." But it quickly became apparent that a mere revision was not sufficient, and that a new concept and Constitution would be required.

---

* After the war, a group of officers, long unpaid and frustrated by Congress' delay in concluding peace, were planning a mutiny, and circulated a petition among their colleagues for support. Washington learned of the plot and called the officers together. He had prepared an address denouncing the conspirators, but as he faced his men, he faltered and fumbled for his spectacles. "Gentlemen," he appealed, "You will permit me to put my glasses on, for I have not only grown gray but almost blind in your service." Tears came to the eyes of many of the officers, and no further word was necessary from Washington for all thought of mutiny to be given up.[14]

** "It may be asked whether history has not vindicated in Washington the doctrine that 'whosoever would be first among you, shall be the servant of all.' "

DOUGLAS SOUTHALL FREEMAN[15]

64

Unity of aim and mutual trust were essential if differences were to be resolved and the nation launched upon its independent course.

A test of leadership is the capacity to inspire men of different, even contrary, characters and capacities to work together toward a common goal. The 55 delegates from twelve states at Philadelphia displayed a diversity of talent, scholarship and experience as well as goodwill, and all these elements were indispensable to the formation of the new government.* Although Washington made not a single major speech during the four months he presided over the sessions, there can be little doubt that it was his character and the universal confidence placed in him by the delegates which was the "headstone and corner" of the Constitution.** "Be assured," wrote James Monroe to Jefferson in Paris, "his influence carried this government."

After the Constitution had been ratified by nine States, the country turned once again to George Washington, who alone, "by the authority of his name and the confidence reposed in his perfect integrity,"[18] was deemed capable of directing the new government.† Both times unanimously elected, he served two terms as President of the United States and drew some of the ablest men of the country into his Cabinet, where, for example, Thomas Jefferson and Alexander Hamilton worked together in spite of deep personal and political differences.

As President, George Washington took courageous, prece-

* The meetings of the Delegates were private. Not a word of their deliberations was leaked to the public while they remained in session. And "the fact that the country did not complain of this secrecy is the best proof of the confidence felt in the members of the Convention."
JAMES BRYCE—1888
** "If to please the people," replied Washington to a question of principle, "we offer that which we ourselves disapprove, how can we afterwards defend our work? Let us raise a standard to which the wise and honest can repair. The event is in the hand of God."[17]
† "The confidence of the whole nation is centered in you," wrote Thomas Jefferson to Washington. "North and South will hang together if they have you to hang on."[19]

dent-setting decisions, organized the machinery of government and established the Republic in the hearts of his countrymen. He steadfastly maintained his aim of creating a national character which would win the respect and emulation of other nations.[20]

George Washington's source of power was most certainly a simple faith in "Divine Providence," and a life committed to great purposes.* He saw God's Hand in history, and could look "with a kind of pious exultation" at the evidences of His favor toward America.[22] In the Army, the General's orders had included "punctual attendance at Divine Services," not as a formality but to implore the blessings of heaven "upon the means used for our safety and defense."** As President, Washington proclaimed a national Thanksgiving Day, formerly a local New England celebration. He was a devout man who, we are told, conducted his private devotions daily,[23] and among his papers was to be found a little book of prayers in his own handwriting.

Washington kneeling in the snow at Valley Forge remains a symbol of the faith that created and sustains America.

At the end of his second term as President, Washington refused to seek a third term, although repeatedly urged to do so, and certain of re-election if he did. He thereby established a precedent which was followed for 144 years and subsequently made a part of the law of the land by the 25th Amendment to the Constitution. He attended the Inauguration of his successor, John Adams, and returned to his beloved Mt. Vernon. There, in the bosom of his family, he cultivated his farms, exchanged visits with his neighbors and kept in touch with events through correspondence and

* "Belief in God and trust in His overruling power formed the essence of his (Washington's) character," wrote the historian George Bancroft. "His whole being was one continued act of faith in the eternal, intelligent and moral order of the universe."[21]

** "While we are duly performing our duty of good soldiers, we ought not to be inattentive to the higher duties of religion. To the distinguished character of a Patriot, it should be our higher glory to add the more distinguished character of a Christian."

To The Army—May, 1778

66

the many friends and visitors who were entertained at the hospitable Washington home.

A year after his retirement, when war with France threatened, Washington yielded to the entreaties of his countrymen and accepted appointment as Commander-in-Chief of a provisional Army. Happily, the crisis passed and he was not called upon for further active national service. On December 14, 1799, he died at his Mount Vernon home of a throat infection contracted while inspecting his farm.

On the news of George Washington's death, the whole United States mourned him as a father. Congress adjourned, and next day John Marshall, Representative from Virginia and later Chief Justice of the United States, rose in the Chamber and read certain Resolutions. These had been prepared by Washington's old friend and colleague, Colonel Henry Lee. They concluded:

> RESOLVED: that a joint committee of both Houses be appointed to report measures suitable to the occasion and expressive of the profound sorrow with which the Congress is penetrated on the loss of a citizen, first in war, first in peace, first in the hearts of his countrymen.[24]

Each year, the U.S. Congress assembles to hear read George Washington's Farewell Address. In this, the Father of his Country sums up his convictions and hopes for the American people whom he served so faithfully. His prayer is that America, blest possessor of liberty, will so cherish and share this blessing that all nations may look to her as an inspiration and example.*

---

* When the news of America's loss crossed the Atlantic, it brought forth an outpouring of tribute from Europe as well. "The whole range of history," editorialized the *Morning Chronicle* of London, "does not present to our view a character upon which we can dwell with such entire and unmixed admiration. The long life of General Washington is not stained by a single blot. . . . His fame, bounded by no country, will be confined to no age."

At Brest, where a British fleet was blockading, ensigns were dipped to half-mast. Napoleon Bonaparte ordered a requiem of ten days in France, and delivered a eulogy in person at the Temple of Mars in Paris.

CHAPTER X

John Adams

No one contributed more to the American
Revolution from the beginning to the end.[1]
LA ROCHEFOUCAULD—1795

JOHN Adams was born in 1735 on a farm in Braintree, near
Boston. His family had lived in Massachusetts for several
generations. His father was determined that young John
should be educated at Harvard College and enter the Congregational ministry. John, however, wanted to be a farmer.
He hated school and might have ended up as an early
American drop-out had it not been for a tutor who encouraged him to find an interest in his studies and make up his
work. John entered Harvard when he was sixteen years old
and graduated four years later.

But John felt no calling to the ministry. He taught
school, studied law, and was admitted to the bar. In the
legal profession, a keen mind and hard work brought him
increasing prominence. Much of the Revolutionary leadership would be drawn from this field, and John Adams was
one of the first to understand the issues underlying the
approaching conflict between Great Britain and her American colonies. He early took the radical position that Parliament had no authority whatsoever to levy taxes upon colonists who were not represented in that body;[2] that these
had a right to liberty "derived from our Maker."[3] Rulers,
moreover, were no more than "agents and trustees" for the
people. Adams' speeches and writings helped to focus colo-

69

nial opposition to the Stamp Act and other unpopular measures of the British Government.

John had married Abigail Smith, daughter of a popular minister. They established their first home in Braintree. Within a few years, his law practice increasing and he himself drawn more and more into public affairs, John moved his family to Boston, where he soon became a leader of the Massachusetts Whigs and a force in the "liberty movement."

John Adams' radical views and growing influence became a concern to the British Government. In an effort to win him over, an offer of a judgeship was made. Young and ambitious, with a family to support, John nevertheless turned his back upon a tempting opportunity for advancement, and replied to this bid with a firm "No!"

A further test of John's mettle was soon to come. Popular antagonism against British soldiers quartered in the town at this time exploded in a riot. A unit of British soldiers was attacked by a mob. Shots were fired, and five citizens killed in what came to be called "The Boston Massacre." A captain and eight soldiers were arraigned on a charge of murder. In the atmosphere of public hostility engendered by this incident, no lawyer could be found to represent the accused. As a last resort, John Adams was approached.

Adams was convinced the soldiers were innocent of the charge, and had fired in self-defense. Acting, as he wrote in his diary, "in a sense of duty," he took the case.[4] In so doing, John invited not only the contempt and criticism of his fellow-patriots but, what was worse, the approbation of the Tories. He risked his safety as well as his reputation. He was jostled in the street, found himself the target of mud-balls, and had stones thrown through his windows. Nevertheless, he got the soldiers acquitted.

Soon after this episode, a seat became vacant in the Massachusetts legislature. John, on the suggestion of his cousin Sam Adams, decided "against his own judgment"[5] to stand for election. Whatever damage his reputation had suffered as a result of his defense of the British soldiers proved to be temporary, for John Adams was elected by a large majority. As the colonies drew together in the face of British coercive measures, John was chosen as a Delegate to the Continental Congress. It was while in Philadelphia that he began the correspondence with Abigail, back home with the children in Massachusetts, which has left posterity an intimate picture of the life and times of this American family and of the sacrifices these men and women made in serving their countrymen.

John Adams was a lawyer and his ambition had been directed toward success in his profession. He lacked the common touch of his cousin Sam, and had an aversion to politics. Yet he seemed drawn by a kind of destiny into political activity, and at every stage of the unfolding confrontation with Britain his moral conviction, courage and articulate grasp of basic principles made him indispensable to the American cause.

In Philadelphia, where the Delegates were divided by sectional and ideological issues, John Adams was "The Atlas of Independence"[6]—a "Colossus on the floor of Congress,"[7] whose eloquence and passion could move the Members from their seats and, more important, unite them in support of revolutionary measures. Appointed to serve on a committee of five to draw up a Declaration of Independence, John urged a fellow committee-member, Thomas Jefferson, to write the document, and Jefferson agreed provided Adams would support it in the Congress.

And support it he did. "Sink or swim, live or die, survive or perish, I give my hand and my heart to this vote," declared Adams to the Delegates. "Before God I believe the hour has come. My judgment approves this measure, and my whole heart is in it; all that I have and all that I am, and all that I hope in this life, I am now ready here to stake upon it! Independence *now* and INDEPENDENCE FOREVER!"

After the Declaration was signed, John wrote to his wife,

telling her the momentous news and concluding that "a greater question perhaps never was nor will be decided among men." He continued as a Member of the Continental Congress, where he was appointed head of the Board of War and Ordnance and served on numerous committees, until he was elected to supersede Silas Deane as American Commissioner to France.*

In 1778, Adams slipped through the British naval blockade of Boston and sailed for Europe on the first of the journeys which in the next few years were to take him to France, Holland and England on historic missions.**

During this period he took part, with Benjamin Franklin and others, in negotiations which secured recognition of the United States by France and The Netherlands together with indispensable financial aid for the embattled Americans. In England, John Adams' work was effective in creating a section of public opinion favorable to America, and at the close of the war he was appointed first United States Minister to Great Britain.

Between European journeys, John Adams served on a commission to draft a Constitution for Massachusetts. This code, much of which comes from his pen, remains today the organic law of the Commonwealth. At the request of George Wythe, he assisted in framing the Constitution of Virginia, and helped as well with identical projects for North Carolina, New York and New Jersey.

In 1787, John Adams was in England and unable to attend the Convention which was meeting during that summer in Philadelphia. From his London diplomatic post, however, he published a work entitled, "A Defense of the Constitutions and Government of the United States," which gave direction and support to the work of the Dele-

* During his years in the Congress, John Adams was a member of 90 committees and chairman of 25.

** John was accompanied on this trip by his eldest son, John Quincy Adams, then only ten years old, who spent many of his subsequent early years gaining precocious diplomatic experience in Europe.

gates. This "gift to his country" was judged "to have done more service than if he had obtained alliances with all the nations of Europe."[8] For it was John Adams' conviction that "a legislative, executive and judicial power comprehend the whole of what is meant and understood by government,"[9] and this principle of the separation of powers became embodied in the Constitution of the United States.*

With the Constitution ratified and the new Government established, John Adams was elected Vice-President of the United States under Washington, and eight years later followed him in the Presidency as candidate of the Federalist Party.

During President Adams' Administration, he strove to maintain George Washington's policy of building "a national character of our own." Like Washington, he hated party strife, which he associated with "the spirit of sophistry . . . intrigue, profligacy and corruption" as natural enemies of the Constitution.[11] Nevertheless, the United States was increasingly drawn into the European vortex which followed upon the French Revolution. The President with difficulty was able to keep the country free from entanglement in the current conflict between France and Great Britain, with both powers indifferent to American rights. Moreover, political parties had begun to play their role in America; Adams himself had been elected by a margin of only three electoral votes. The Federalist Party was split, the political tides turned against them, and Adams was defeated for a second term by Thomas Jefferson and the Republican-Democrats.

John Adams had fought in the front rank of his country's political and ideological struggles, but his fundamental battle was with himself. His early resolve to "conquer (my) natural pride and conceit; subdue every unworthy passion," is recorded in his diary, and it was without doubt this

* "That power might be abused," explained John Marshall, "was deemed conclusive reason why it should not be conferred."[10]

struggle for self-mastery which bred in John a conviction that "public virtue" must be the heart of the Republic. He sometimes doubted if America possessed sufficient of this quality to support a republic, yet he was convinced that it was the duty of a political leader to help shape the character of the people.[12]

John Adams had a deep respect for women, whose manners, he was convinced, are "the most infallible barometer" of a nation's moral climate.[13] He was a "family man" who believed, nevertheless, that family life should be not without "a very extensive connection with society at large" and with the broad public interest.[14] His wife, Abigail, when not with him in London or Paris during his long absences from home, brought up their four children, ran the farm and conducted his business. Abigail was a competent manager and a shrewd judge of people, writing to her husband astute comments on national policies and personalities as well as news of the family and local affairs.* He in turn kept his wife abreast of current events and issues. From Philadelphia, for example, he wrote her that the appointment of the "most virtuous, the amiable and generous and brave George Washington" as General of the American Army would be effective in "cementing and securing the union" of the colonies.

The Adams letters were not restricted to news and personalities. "I know I have a right to your whole heart," Abigail wrote to John, "because my own never knew another lord."[16] John in turn assured her that not an hour of the day went by in which he did not think of her "with every sentiment of tender feeling."[17]

John indeed could look back over his family's adventures and "see a kind of romance" which, embellished with a little "poetical ornament, would equal anything in the days of chivalry or knight errantry."[18] The pressure of daily problems and the hurt of separation are not passed over,

---

* Abigail reported to her husband her impression of Benjamin Franklin, whom she met at a dinner party, as "a patriot and a Christian," and added that "a true patriot must be a religious man."[15]

74

but Abigail can tell her husband that she finds joy in mutual sacrifice with one who is "worthy of the important trust devolved upon him."[19]* As Vice-President, John complains to Abigail that his office is "the most insignificant that ever the invention of man contrived or his imagination conceived." On his election to the Presidency, he must have been heartened by her "petitions to heaven . . . that the things that make for peace may not be hidden from you."

Abigail's letter of condolence to Thomas Jefferson upon the death of his daughter Mary, who had lived in the Adams home in London, helped re-establish the friendship, sadly interrupted by party divisions, between the families.

John Adams lived to the age of 90 and in retirement maintained contact from his Braintree home with a host of friends and public men. He carried on a voluminous correspondence with Jefferson, who outlived him by only a few hours. They died on the same day, July 4, 1826, the anniversary of the signing of the Declaration of Independence which both had fathered in the Congress fifty years before. A celebration had been planned in Braintree and, a few days earlier, John Adams received a request to send a communication to the assemblage. He replied with a two-word message: "INDEPENDENCE FOREVER!"

John Quincy Adams, eldest son of John and Abigail, became the sixth President of the United States, and their descendants have included many distinguished statesmen, authors and civic figures.**

* Asked by a Braintree Selectman, "If you had known that Mr. Adams would have remained so long abroad, would you have consented that he should have gone?" Abigail, after a moment's reflection, replied: "If I had known, sir, that Mr. Adams could have effected what he has done, I would not only have submitted to the absence I have endured, painful as it has been, but I would not have opposed it even though three years more should be added to the number, which Heaven avert! I feel a pleasure in being able to sacrifice my selfish passions to the general good, and in imitating the example which has taught me to consider myself and family but as the small dust of the balance when compared with the great community."[20]
** See Appendix V.

CHAPTER XI

Thomas Jefferson

> All honor to Jefferson, to the man who . . . had the cool-
> ness, forecast and capacity to introduce into a mere revo-
> lutionary document an abstract truth, applicable to all
> men and all times.
>
> ABRAHAM LINCOLN—1859[1]

A passion for the freedom of the human spirit burned in Thomas Jefferson.* Farmer, philosopher, architect, athlete, inventor, musician, educator, diplomat, scholar, statesman—perhaps no man's ideas have had more influence upon American democracy.

One of the youngest of the Founding Fathers, Thomas Jefferson was born April 13, 1743, on a tobacco plantation in Albemarle County, at that time a frontier of the Blue Ridge in Virginia. His father, Peter Jefferson, was a man of unusual strength and enterprise, landowner, civil engineer, Colonel of Militia and Member of the House of Burgesses. As County Surveyor, he made the first map of Virginia.

Thomas' mother was a Randolph, one of the first families of the colony.

His father died when Thomas was fourteen years old, leaving his son a substantial property. He had also seen to it that Tom attended a local school where he studied the

---

* "I have sworn upon the altar of God," wrote Jefferson, "eternal hostility against every form of tyranny over the mind of man."[2]

classics at an early age. Entering William and Mary College, Tom graduated with a good knowledge of Latin,
Greek and French, to which he later added Spanish, Italian
and Anglo-Saxon, as well as acquiring familiarity with
higher mathematics and natural sciences. He studied law
under the eminent George Wythe, was admitted to the bar,
and two years later entered the House of Burgesses.

Thus from his youth Thomas Jefferson was recognized
as a leader in Virginia, the oldest, largest and wealthiest
of the Colonies. While still in his twenties, he took part in
producing the "Virginia Resolves," asserting the Colony's
right to be taxed only by its own representatives. He helped
organize "Committees of Correspondence" throughout the
colonies, and was a founder of the "Non-Importation Association," which initiated a boycott in Virginia of British
goods.

In 1772, Thomas Jefferson married Martha Skelton, and
they established their home at "Monticello," the beautiful
mansion he designed and built on his plantation near
Charlottesville.

At the age of 32, Jefferson was elected a Delegate to the
Continental Congress, where his reputation as a political
thinker entitled him to be chosen as a member of the committee to draw up the Declaration of Independence. It was
Jefferson's draft, with a few alterations by the Congress
(including deletion of a section proscribing slavery) which
was signed by the Delegates on July 4, 1776.

The Declaration was the decisive step by which the
colonies severed their political connection with England.
In it, Jefferson and the revolutionary leaders not only con-
demned the abuses they were fighting against, but proclaimed the principles they were fighting for. They made
clear that these principles were the "unalienable rights" of
all mankind. It was this objective which united the colonies, and at the same time won strong support in Britain
itself, where eminent figures like Pitt and Burke hailed the

American challenge as an expression of the true heritage of British liberties.*

The Declaration of Independence has taken its place as one of the title-deeds of human freedom.

In the Fall of 1776, Jefferson returned to the Virginia legislature where he was appointed member of a commission to revise the laws and constitution of the State. It was here that he promoted some of the most advanced, democratic measures of the time. These included repeal of the archaic statutes governing inheritance and land tenure, bills to support public education, and the landmark "Statute of Virginia for Religious Freedom." His bill to allow owners to free their slaves failed of support, but Jefferson continued steadfast in his opposition to "this abomination"[4] which he was convinced boded disaster for both races.** "Nothing is more clearly written in the book of fate," he maintained, "than that these people are to be free."[6]

Succeeding Patrick Henry as Governor in 1779, Jefferson worked tirelessly to mobilize Virginia's resources in support of the war effort, and thereby drew from General Washington an expression of warmest appreciation for the "readiness and zeal" with which he had promoted measures recommended by the Commander-in-Chief during a difficult period of the conflict.[7]

In congress once again after the war, Jefferson made the

* "We cannot falsify the pedigree of this fierce people. An Englishman is the unfittest person on earth to argue another Englishman into slavery."   EDMUND BURKE—1775[3]

** Jefferson's opposition to slavery was based on his conviction that freedom is the God-given right of all men. "And can the liberties of a nation be thought secure," he queried, "when we have removed their only firm basis, a conviction in the minds of the people that these liberties are the gifts of God?" In the same passage, he warned, "Indeed I tremble for my country when I reflect that God is just; that his justice cannot sleep forever." What must come, Jefferson prophesied, was "a total emancipation," which he hoped would be "with the consent of the masters rather than their extirpation."[5]

proposal and plan on which our present system of coinage is based, and drew up an ordinance for the government of the western territories of the United States, forerunner of the notable "Northwest Ordinance" of 1787.* His hopes of retiring to Monticello at this point were interrupted by his appointment as minister plenipotentiary, with John Adams and Benjamin Franklin, to negotiate treaties of commerce with European governments. He joined Franklin in Paris, and the following year was appointed United States Minister to France.**

In France, where the republican Jefferson was popular and highly respected in liberal circles, he published his famous *Notes on Virginia*. His friendship with Lafayette opened many democratic doors, and he was even invited to help draft a constitution for the National Assembly. Returning to America after witnessing the outbreak of the French Revolution, Jefferson was considered to have achieved an outstanding success in his diplomatic post.†

The following year, Jefferson accepted President Washington's invitation to join his cabinet as Secretary of State. Later he was to serve his country as Vice President and for two terms as President (1801–1809), his years of public service extending over a span of more than four decades.

In Washington's cabinet a fellow-member with Jefferson was Alexander Hamilton, the brilliant and able Secretary of the Treasury. Born in the West Indies, Hamilton favored a strong central government with power concentrated in a commercial class and exercised by "the rich and well-born."[9]

* Daniel Webster doubted "whether one single law of any lawgiver, ancient or modern, has produced effects more distinct, marked or of lasting character."[8]

** "It is you who replace Dr. Franklin?" Jefferson was asked in Paris. "No one can replace him," he replied, "I am only his successor."

† Even the critical *Edinburgh Review*, in 1789, admitted that "the skill and knowledge with which he argued the different questions of national interest that arose during his residence will not suffer even in comparison with Franklin's diplomatic talents."

During the war, he had been an aide to Washington, who relied strongly upon his financial and political acumen.

Jefferson recognized "a natural aristocracy," but it would be based on "virtue and talent"—not wealth.[10] Moreover, he mistrusted centralized government, and had no faith in an industrial society with its rootless, urban proletariat. He envisaged rather a nation of small landholders ("the most precious part of the state")[11] as the soil to nourish democracy and its freedoms.

Opposition between the two men was inevitable, and it came to a head over the question of payment of the States' Revolutionary War debts. The breach widened under the impact of the French Revolution upon American sympathies and the threat of United States involvement in a European war. Cabinet meetings were stormy. Both men controlled newspapers, which supported opposing sides. Public opinion became noisily divided over the issues. More than once, Jefferson decided to resign from the cabinet, but each time Washington persuaded him to stay on.

By Washington's second term, two factions had already developed on the American political scene. Jefferson was recognized as the father of the Republican (later, Democratic) Party, in opposition to Hamilton and the Federalists. In 1793, Jefferson resigned from the cabinet and retired to his Virginia home.

Thomas Jefferson's wife, Martha, had died in 1782. Their marriage had been a singularly happy one, but only two of their six children lived to grow up, and her death after ten years was a loss which weighed upon him through the rest of his life.

After his wife's death, Jefferson had put his two daughters in a convent school in Paris, where he could keep a fatherly eye on them and provide counsel and encouragement. "It is part of the American character," he reminds Martha (named for her mother), "to surmount every difficulty by resolution and contrivance." His expectations for

THOMAS JEFFERSON

her are high, but not higher than she can attain. "Industry
and resolution are all that are wanting."[12]*

Martha, after she married, made a home for her father
at Monticello, where he found delight in his library and
his garden, experimented with crop-rotation and his latest
inventions—a new clock, a "dumb waiter," a mouldboard
plow. Here he worked over his plans for the University of
Virginia, the site of which he could see from his terrace.
And here, as always, he entertained a procession of friends,
neighbors, and visitors from far and near. From the emi-
nence of his "Little Mountain," Jefferson looked out over
the Virginia countryside he loved. He rode horseback every
day, often accompanied by his young friend and disciple
James Madison who lived nearby. Madison promoted Jefferson's policies at Williamsburg and in the Congress, and
would succeed him in the Presidency.

While at Monticello, Jefferson was quietly mending his
political fences. Four years later, he was back in Washington, having been elected Vice President under John Adams.
In 1801, with the final defeat of the Federalists, he became
President of the United States.**

As President, Jefferson took the bold step, not expressly
authorized by the Constitution, of acquiring from France
for fifteen million dollars the enormous territory included
in the "Louisiana Purchase." With the expedition of Lewis
and Clark (1804)—the first recorded passage of white men
across the present northern United States—the way was
opened for America's expansion as a Continental nation.

During his eight-year tenure of office, Thomas Jefferson

* A month later, Jefferson writes to his daughter again, proposing:
"If you ever find yourself in difficulty and doubt how to extricate
yourself, do what is right, and you will find it the easiest way of
getting out of your difficulty." And the father adds, "Do it for . . .
increasing the happiness of him who loves you infinitely."[13]

** Vice President Jefferson lived in a Washington boarding house,
where he was in the habit of sitting at the foot of the table. On the
day of his Inaugural as President, he rode alone to the Capitol, clad
in a plain suit, so the story goes, tied his horse to a fence, and walked
to the Senate Chamber to read his address.

advanced the country steadily along the course of democratic development, while at the same time maintaining the
character and spirit of the Chief Executives who had preceded him.

Following the precedent set by George Washington, Jefferson declined to seek a third term. In 1809, he returned
for the last time to Monticello where his daughter Martha,
with her eleven children, presided over the hospitable home.
Statesman, scholar, scientist, friend of the people—Thomas
Jefferson was sought out by friends and public figures from
America and Europe who came to pay him homage and seek
counsel from "The Sage of Monticello."* James Madison
and James Monroe continued to consult him on matters of
policy (the "Monroe Doctrine" for example) and thus assured, through the succeeding twenty-four years of their
combined administrations, the continuance of the "Jefferson System."

In the midst of the goings and comings at Monticello, as
well as under the cares of office, Jefferson managed to carry
on a vast correspondence, and sixteen thousand of his letters
are preserved today. These often reveal a particular concern
for younger relatives and friends. A favorite nephew is
urged to apply himself to his studies, as a preparation for
public life, "with the strictest integrity and most chaste
honor."[14] And a year before his death, he admonishes his
namesake, Thomas Jefferson Smith, "Adore God, reverence
and cherish your parents. Love your neighbor as yourself
and your country more than yourself. Be just. Murmur not
at the ways of Providence." And in concluding he suggests,
"When angry, count ten before you speak; if very angry,
a hundred."[15]**

* So generously did Jefferson entertain, and so little attention
had he been able, during his years of public service, to give to his
personal business that he was threatened with bankruptcy after his
retirement. He was forced to sell his library, and only a public sub-
scription saved "Monticello" from the auctioneer's hammer.

** Jefferson was a student of the New Testament, from which he
transcribed Jesus' words into a separate volume ("The Jefferson

One of Thomas Jefferson's last achievements, regarded by him as "the crowning event" of his life, was the founding of the University of Virginia. He worked on the plans, superintended construction, selected the professors, prescribed courses of study, and served for seven years, until his death, on the Board of Visitors. Over a period, he invited each one of the first class of students to dine with him at Monticello.

Up to the end, Thomas Jefferson cherished the hours he could devote to his letters, his library, his farm. He rose early ("The sun has not caught me in bed for fifty years," he said), and in his eighties he still rode horseback ten miles a day.

On June 24, 1826, Jefferson declined an invitation to attend a celebration in Washington of the 50th Anniversary of the signing of the Declaration of Independence. Ten days later on July 4th, he died.

Governor, Ambassador, Cabinet Member and twice President of the United States—Thomas Jefferson's epitaph, which he wrote himself, reads simply:

"Here was buried Thomas Jefferson, Author of the Declaration of American Independence, of the Statute of Virginia for Religious Freedom and Father of the University of Virginia."

Bible"). He regarded himself as "a real Christian," and believed that the nation's "controversy" with Great Britain had been successfully concluded only through Providential intervention.[16] In his official messages as President, he did not neglect to remind the American people of the Source to which they owed the peace and prosperity which they currently enjoyed.[17]

CHAPTER XII

Benjamin Franklin

The greatest man and ornament of the age and country
in which he lived.*

THOMAS JEFFERSON—1798[1]

BENJAMIN Franklin was 70 years old when the Declaration
of Independence was signed, and over eighty when he
took part in the debates at the Constitutional Convention.
His signature appears also upon the Treaty of Alliance
with France, the Treaty of Peace with England and the
Constitution of the United States. He is the only one of the
Founding Fathers to have put his name to all four of the
great State papers which mark the birth of the Republic.

Born in Boston, where his father was a candlemaker,
Ben was the tenth son (fifteenth of seventeen children) in
the family. His parents, hopeful of a career in the ministry,
sent him to grammar school at the age of eight, but could
not afford to keep him there. When he was ten years old,
Ben left school and went to work with his father in the
candle shop.

With his formal schooling concluded, Ben's education
had barely begun. An omnivorous reader, he saved his lunch
money to buy books, and would sit up most of the night
to finish a borrowed volume. He taught himself arithmetic

* "Eripuit coelo fulmen mox scepto tyrannis" (He snatched the
lightning from the sky and the sceptre from tyrants), the Latin inscription attributed to Turgot, is carved on the bust of Franklin made by
Houdon in Paris.

and geography, studied English grammar, and perfected his style of writing by perusing English magazines.

At twelve years of age, Ben Franklin was apprenticed to his half brother, James, who operated a printing shop in Boston. James Franklin published a newspaper, *The New England Courant*, in which a series of controversial articles entitled the "Dogood Letters," authored anonymously by Ben, attracted unfavorable attention from the authorities. James' paper was eventually suppressed, and Ben, when he was seventeen years old, parted company with his brother and left Boston.

Ben travelled to Philadelphia and went to work at his trade as a printer. After an unsuccessful venture in England the following year, he returned to Philadelphia, where he established himself in business, married, and ultimately became the First Citizen of the town.

It is revealing of Ben Franklin's character that, throughout his long and distinguished career, he thought of himself always as a printer, and it was during his early years in Philadelphia that he, somewhat jocosely, wrote an epitaph which was eventually cut on his tombstone:

The Body
of
Benjamin Franklin
(Like the cover of an old book
Its contents torn out
And stripped of its lettering and gilding)
Lies here, food for worms.
Yet the work itself shall not be lost;
For it will (as he believed) appear once more;
in a new and more beautiful edition,
Corrected and amended
By the Author.

In Philadelphia, Franklin founded the "Junto," a social and study group out of which developed many of his ideas and enterprises. He bought a newspaper, the *Pennsylvania*

Gazette, in which he promoted the philosophy of frugality and hard work, printed amusing anecdotes and essays as well as excerpts from other "moral writers," and from it was careful to exclude "libelling and personal abuse."

The *Pennsylvania Gazette* achieved the largest circulation in the colonies and Franklin's *Poor Richard's Almanack,* published three years later, became one of the most widely read American periodicals.*

As a boy, Ben Franklin had read Cotton Mather's *Essays To Do Good,*[2] and his early questionings had given way to certain convictions. He believed that the most acceptable service of God consisted in doing good to one's fellow man; "that our souls are immortal," and that crime would be punished and virtue rewarded, either here or hereafter.**

"Having implored the direction of God," Mather exhorted, "write down your resolutions. A Christian must be no stranger to a course of meditation." Young Franklin rose at five o'clock and engaged in two hours of prayer and meditation to check himself on his standards, and "contrive the day's business." He listed in a notebook thirteen "virtues," wrote down his failures, and prefaced his daily "examination" with a prayer to "the fountain of wisdom." Each night Ben would ask himself, "What good have I done this day?" and pass his conduct under a searching scrutiny.

* Many of "Poor Richard's" sayings are familiar today and as applicable as when they were written.
   "Early to bed, early to rise,
      makes a man healthy, wealthy and wise."
   "God helps those who help themselves."
   "Time is the stuff of life. Don't waste it." Etc.
In an enlarged edition of the *Almanack,* Franklin proposed a "fast day"—the first to be celebrated in Pennsylvania—which set aside Thursday, January 7, 1748, in which to acknowledge, "dependence upon the Divine Being, to give thanks for the mercies received, and no less to deprecate His judgments and humbly pray for His protection."
** "When I was a boy I met with a book entitled, Essays To Do Good which, I think, was written by your father. It . . . gave me such a turn of thinking, as to have influenced my conduct through life."
BENJAMIN FRANKLIN—*Letter to Dr. Samuel Cotton—1783*

Franklin's "little book" can be seen today in the Huntington Library in California.

It was Franklin's observation, while still in his twenties, that few men in public life are motivated purely by concern for the public good, which led him to conclude the time might be ripe for forming a "United Party for Virtue,"[3] and he conceived the "bold and arduous project" of himself attaining moral perfection. Soon, however, he realized that reason and interest required the support of good habits to insure "uniform rectitude of conduct."[4] Pride, he noted, raised particular obstacles, and even if he should succeed in conquering this formidable adversary, Ben suspected he would be proud of his humility.[5]

Franklin's business in Philadelphia flourished. He established printing enterprises in New York, Charleston and the West Indies, and maintained business connections in most of the colonies. By the time he was forty-two, he was able to retire and devote the rest of his life to public affairs and the service of his country.

The printing shop, to be sure, had not restricted Franklin's wide-ranging interests and activities. He instituted the first circulating library in America, organized the first fire company in Philadelphia, and founded the American Philosophical Society. He printed and distributed the sermons of George Whitefield, and was a trustee of the building which served as the center of the great preacher's work in Philadelphia.

Franklin became more and more involved in colonial affairs. He was elected a Member of the Pennsylvania Assembly and re-elected each term for fourteen years. He served on a commission to settle border disputes with the Indians and drew up the "Albany Plan"—one of the earliest attempts to unite the colonies in common action. He was appointed Deputy Postmaster General for America, and organized the first colony-wide postal service.

During the French and Indian War, Franklin mobilized the defense of the frontier settlements and organized a volunteer militia in Pennsylvania, no easy task in the Quaker colony. He personally guaranteed loans for the transport of supplies of the ill-fated Braddock expedition, and offered to pay for the tea dumped into Boston Harbor, on condition that Parliament would repeal the disputed taxes. During the Revolution, he spent his own money to purchase supplies for the Continental Army.

Ben Franklin's mind was drawn to experiment and investigation of natural phenomena.* He initiated experiments with electricity which led to his famous discovery of the properties of lightning. He invented the Franklin Stove, constructed a mangle (which attracted George Washington's interest), made a pair of bifocal spectacles for his own use, and a harmonica. He wrote about the new technique of inoculation for smallpox,[6] and taught the Pennsylvania farmers to use chemical fertilizers. Franklin followed closely the first experiments with balloons in France,** and once expressed a wish that he might have been born two or three centuries hence, anticipating future advances in science and invention.

As a philosopher and scientist, self-educated Ben Franklin accumulated honors at home and abroad. Harvard and Yale bestowed on him the Degree of Master of Arts; he received Doctor of Laws and Doctor of Civil Laws Degrees from St. Andrews University in Scotland and from Oxford University. The Royal Societies of Edinburgh and Britain extended membership to him. He received the British Society's Copley medal, as well as a letter of commendation from King Louis XV of France.

In 1757, Ben Franklin went to England to represent Pennsylvania in a dispute with the Penn family over taxes. He spent fifteen years in that country as agent for Pennsylvania and other colonies. Franklin had believed that the

---

* As a boy, Ben had impressed his swimming companions by tying a kite to his wrist and letting it pull him through the water.

** Asked, "Of what use is a balloon?" Franklin replied, "Of what use is a new-born baby?"

interests of the British Empire lay in America[7] but, with the passage of the Stamp Act and further blundering by the Parliament, he became convinced that the colonies were destined to become independent. He helped organize a press campaign in Britain for the American cause, and it was Franklin who induced Tom Paine to come to America.

When separation of the colonies from England became inevitable, Franklin returned to America. His wife, Deborah, had died three years before, and Ben took up residence with his daughter Sally Bache and her family in Philadelphia.

Soon elected a member of the Continental Congress, he served on ten committees. The Congress commissioned him as Postmaster General, and he was selected as one of the committee to draft the Declaration of Independence. Not long afterwards, Franklin was chosen as a Commissioner, with John Adams and Arthur Lee, to go to France to solicit financial and military support for the Americans. Two years later, he was appointed Minister to that country.

In France, where he had been made a member of the French Academy of Sciences, Benjamin Franklin enjoyed enormous respect and veneration. The originator of "Poor Richard" was honored in Court circles and soon became the fashion of Paris and a national figure. The Treaty of Alliance which he succeeded in negotiating brought to America a French fleet and army and financial aid which helped assure victory for American arms.*

After signing the Treaty of Peace with Britain, Franklin returned once more to Philadelphia. He was elected a Member of the Executive Council, and President (Governor) of Pennsylvania, and presided over the State's Constitutional Convention. In the midst of multifarious activities, he found time to include among his publications a dissertation, "On the Cause and Cure of Smoky Chimneys" and a work entitled "Maritime Observations" based upon obser-

* "We must have one of two things," wrote George Washington to Franklin in 1780, "Peace, or money from France."

vations of the Gulf Stream during his Atlantic crossings. He also resumed work on his *Autobiography* which he had begun several years earlier.

At the age of eighty-one, Benjamin Franklin took his seat in the Convention called in Philadelphia to revise the "Articles of Confederation" or, as it turned out, to frame a Constitution for the United States. The task of the Convention proved difficult, and without Franklin's wisdom, prestige and tact, might well have proved impossible. At a critical point in their deliberations he proposed that a chaplain be employed and the sessions opened with prayer. "The longer I live," Franklin told the delegates, "the more convincing proofs I see that God governs in the affairs of men"; he recalled the prayers of the Continental Congress during the war, and the evidence that these had been answered. And he concluded that without God's "concurring aid we shall succeed in this political building no better than the builders of Babel."

Franklin himself did not favor certain proposals in the Constitution as drafted, but he was prepared to accept it as the best that their united endeavors could produce, and he cautioned the delegates against permitting personal points of view to undercut their essential work of building foundations for a national government. He appealed to each one who might have reservations to "doubt a little of his own infallibility," and put his name to the document.

Although no action had been taken on his suggestion of recourse to prayer (which some members feared might be construed as an act of desperation), Franklin recognized in the eventual success of the Convention* the Hand of Providence by Whom he believed "the general government"[8] of the world to be conducted, and to Whom he had prayed as a young man for help in his personal moral struggles.

* As the ceremony of the signing drew to a close, Franklin called the delegates' attention to a picture of the sun on the high-backed chair from which George Washington had presided over their sessions. "Now I have the happiness to know," he told them, "it is a rising, not a setting sun."

Benjamin Franklin's long life and manifold achievements contributed enormously to his country's standing in the world community. "While I am writing to the Philosopher and a friend," concluded Dr. Erasmus Darwin, "I cannot forget that I am also writing to the greatest Statesman of the present or perhaps any century, who spread the contagion of Liberty among his countrymen; and like the greatest man of all antiquity, the leader of the Jews, delivered them from the House of Bondage and the scourge of oppression."[9] So wrote the grandfather of Charles Darwin to Benjamin Franklin.

"The first philosopher and indeed the first great man of letters"[10] for whom Europe was beholden to America, Franklin's vision was not limited to his own country.* The United States, he believed, could provide an example and inspiration to Europe, where he envisaged "a Federal union and one grand republic . . . by means of a like Convention."[12]

A scientist to the end, "having seen a good deal of this world," Franklin at eighty years "acknowledged a growing desire to become acquainted with some other. . . ." He remained confident that he could trust his spirit to God, Who had so graciously protected throughout life both him and his country.[13]

Benjamin Franklin died April 17, 1790. His funeral cortege was led by every clergyman—parson, priest and rabbi—in Philadelphia, and half the population of the city took part in or viewed his obsequies.

In France, where he had labored so long and fruitfully for his country, the Chamber of Deputies decreed a three-day period of mourning for Benjamin Franklin.

* In 1789, a year before his death, Franklin wrote to a friend in England, "God grant that not only the love of liberty but a thorough knowledge of the rights of man may pervade all the nations of the earth, so that a philosopher may set his foot anywhere on its surface and say, 'This is my country.'"[11]

CHAPTER XIII

Abraham Lincoln

The grandest figure on the crowded canvas of the drama
of the nineteenth century.

WALT WHITMAN—1865*

AT the time of the Revolution, the original settlements
of the Eastern seaboard had overflowed the Alle-
ghenies, and new settlers, preceded by frontiersmen such as
Daniel Boone, were pouring into the Midwest. By the turn
of the century, the explorers Lewis and Clark had penetrated the Northwest to the Pacific, and, a few years later,
the fur-seeking "Mountain Men" crossed the plains, soon
followed by the covered wagons carrying pioneer families.

In the van of the explorers went priests—Père Marquette
who discovered the Mississippi River, and the Whitmans,
missionary statesmen who helped open the huge territory
of Oregon and Washington.

Hard on the heels of the missionaries, explorers and fur
traders, came the settlers. As land was cleared and cultivated, communities were founded. Soon the western migration from the Eastern seaboard was being swelled by immigrants from across the seas. Many of the new settlers came
direct from Europe, with a sprinkling of Asiatics. Today's

* "I should say that the invisible foundations and vertebra of his
character, more than any man's in history, were . . . moral and
spiritual—while upon all of them were built . . . what the vulgar call
horse sense."

WALT WHITMAN[1]

93

Americans have roots as well in almost every other country on earth.

Out of this new frontier came Abraham Lincoln. Born in the last year of Thomas Jefferson's presidency, Lincoln was to preserve the nation which the Founders built. His family had moved from Virginia to Pennsylvania, then Kentucky, Indiana, Illinois. His father was a farmer, hunter, carpenter. His grandfather had been killed by Indians while working on his farm.

The boy Lincoln went to work in the fields when he was six years old. He used to walk four miles to school, and he studied his lessons by firelight, writing with a piece of charcoal on a wooden shovel.

Lincoln's mother, who could not read or write, used to tell him Bible stories from memory. In later years at the White House, he often kept an open Bible on his desk.

At seventeen years of age, young Abe was six feet four inches tall and the best axeman, runner and wrestler in the region. When he was twenty-two, he took a trip to New Orleans, traveling down the Mississippi by flatboat. It was on this trip that he saw slaves being advertised for sale in the market. The sight sickened him. "It run its iron into him then and there," a friend recalled.[2]*

Lincoln left the farm and kept a store in Illinois. Although he attended school less than a year in his whole life, he was an avid reader and studied law and the English classics in his spare time. Soon he went into law practice with a partner.

At twenty-three, Lincoln made his first political speech. He was elected to the Illinois State Legislature, where he served four terms, and to a term in the United States House of Representatives. In Congress, Lincoln introduced a resolution for the eventual abolition of slavery in the District of Columbia, but it was not adopted.

* Memories of a party of "ten or a dozen slaves shackled together with irons," with whom he had traveled to St. Louis by steamboat in 1841, remained "a continual torment" to Lincoln.[3]

During Lincoln's last term in the Legislature, he married Mary Todd, daughter of a prominent Kentucky family. She was an able, ambitious woman who had a remarkable insight into Lincoln's character and destiny. She always believed he would be President one day. They had four sons, two of whom survived him.

Meanwhile the issues dividing the country grew more critical. The Missouri Compromise, a statute enacted in 1820 limiting the extension of slavery, was superseded by the Kansas-Nebraska law which opened the western territory to the South's "peculiar institution." Bloody conflict exploded between pro and anti-slavery settlers. John Brown's raid fanned the flames of sectional hatred. The Boston abolitionist William Lloyd Garrison publicly burned a copy of the United States Constitution, crying, "So perish all compromises with tyranny!"* The book *Uncle Tom's Cabin*, dramatizing the evils of slavery, sold a million copies in the North.

Lincoln ran for the United States Senate against Stephen A. Douglas, sponsor of the Kansas-Nebraska Law, and although defeated he gained national prominence through his debates with Douglas during the campaign. Four years later, he was elected President of the United States.

As President, Lincoln found himself the head of "a house divided against itself."[4] He was faced with the "irrepressible conflict,"[5] and knew he was powerless to stop it. "I am in the garden of Gethsemane," he confessed to a friend.[6] For this public ordeal, Lincoln had been prepared by the tragedies which had darkened his personal life. He lost his mother when he was ten years old, and a few years later his sister died. His first engagement was broken by the death of his fiancée. Two sons died, one in the second year of his Presidency, when the added burden of his loss proved almost too heavy to bear.

* Under Garrison's leadership, the Massachusetts Anti-Slavery Society resolved, as early as 1843, that the U.S. Constitution was "A covenant with death and an agreement with hell." (Isaiah 18,15)

Lincoln was struck by the paradox of two antagonists praying to the same God.[7] Yet he himself spent much time in prayer, and felt God's hand upon him during these trials. He expressed an "earnest desire" to know the will of Providence. "I talk to God," he said, "and a way is suggested that always accords with a commonsense view of the work."[8]

With The Bible and *Pilgrim's Progress*, Lincoln's only boyhood reading had been the lives of Washington and Franklin. Their example inspired and strengthened him. Facing his first term in the Presidency, Lincoln compared his task with Washington's. "I feel that I cannot succeed without the same divine aid which sustained him" he told his Illinois supporters on leaving for the nation's capital, "and on that same Almighty Being I place my reliance for support."[9]

In a General Order to the Army, President Lincoln repeated General Washington's direction to the officers and men of the Continental troops to conduct themselves as "Christian soldiers defending their country."[10]

President Lincoln's "paramount object" was "not either to save or to destroy slavery" but to "save the Union."[11] Nevertheless, his political life had been built upon opposition to slavery, which he termed a "monstrous evil." In his debates with Douglas, he had more than once invoked the Declaration of Independence and challenged the electorate to "re-adopt" both the Charter itself and "practices and policy which harmonize with it."*

Under increasing wartime pressures, Abraham Lincoln never forgot that he was President of the whole nation, and

* ". . . slavery . . . a monstrous evil. . . . Let us re-adopt the Declaration of Independence. . . .

"If we do this, we shall not only have saved the Union, but shall have so saved it as to make and keep it forever worthy of saving. We shall have so saved it that the succeeding millions of free, happy people, the world over, shall rise up and call us blessed to the latest generation."[12]

ABRAHAM LINCOLN—1854

he refused to be swept from that position by the storms of hatred and controversy that raged about him. He had done everything he could, consistent with his oath of office, to avert the war. "We are not enemies but friends," he pleaded in his First Inaugural Address. "We must not be enemies."[13] During the war, Lincoln spoke of "the enemy, who is of our own household."[14] And when one of his Generals made use of the phrase "driving the invaders from our soil," he said he wished our generals would get that idea out of their heads, "The whole country is our soil," he insisted.[15]

In the North, public opinion had been far from united in support of the war. Faith in military leaders was shaken by unexpected Southern victories. Personal and political rivalries hampered the government. Vicious press attacks were launched against the President. Draft riots broke out in New York. On January 1, 1863, Lincoln issued the Emancipation Proclamation and, the following summer, with Union victories at Gettysburg and Vicksburg, the tide appeared to have turned. Yet almost two more years were to pass, and President Lincoln would begin his second term, before the South would yield to the overwhelming force and resources of the Union.

The Bible had nourished young Lincoln's mind and it strengthened him through mature trials. There is a prophetic note in many of his public utterances, and this is nowhere more apparent than in his Second Inaugural Address. "The Almighty has His own purposes,"[16] the President reminded his countrymen. Recalling the Scriptural warning that "offenses must come, but woe to that man by whom the offense cometh," Lincoln points to American slavery as one of the offenses, and the war, for which both North and South are held accountable, as one of the woes inflicted by a just God upon the offenders.* He closes with the immortal challenge:

* Matthew 18,7. One recalls the forebodings about slavery of Thomas Jefferson, who wrote: "This momentous question (The Missouri Com-

"With malice toward none, with charity for all, with firmness in the right as God gives us to see the right, let us strive on to finish the work we are in . . . To do all that may achieve and cherish a just and lasting peace among ourselves and with all nations."

Amid the cares of office, President Lincoln maintained his humanity, humility and a robust sense of humor. When urged to couch his State papers in more formal language, he explained that if they were simple the people would understand. Hearing himself described as "common-looking," the President remarked, "The Lord prefers common-looking people; that is the reason He makes so many of them." When someone told him that General Grant was said to have weakness for liquor, Lincoln, who did not drink himself, asked what kind of whiskey Grant used, and declared he would like to send some to his other Generals.

To a friend who reported that a certain Senator Sherman had prepared a speech critical of Lincoln, the President replied that Sherman was a patriot, and might be right in his criticism; Lincoln would not have him change a word. Sherman heard about the President's reaction, and deleted the criticism.

Lincoln was no stranger to honest apology when he felt he had made a mistake. After a disagreement with Grant in regard to the Vicksburg campaign, the President wrote him: "I wish to make the personal acknowledgement that you were right and I was wrong."[18] He could, on the other hand, deal trenchantly with a self-important officer who importuned him for a higher command.*

promise) like a fire-bell in the night, awakened and filled me with terror. I considered it at once as the knell of the Union. It is hushed, indeed, for the moment. But this is a reprieve only. . . ."[17]

* Lincoln warned this officer that he was adopting the best possible way to ruin himself, and pointed out that a man "who does something at the head of one regiment," will outshine him who "does nothing at the head of 100."[19]

Abraham Lincoln's concern for the common soldier was legendary, and in the War Department files are scores of telegrams, and letters in the President's hand granting pardon or amnesty to various offenders. To a General who urged him to sign an order for the execution of a young Union soldier who had fallen asleep on sentry duty, Lincoln retorted that there were already too many weeping widows in the land. "Do not ask me to add to their number," he replied, "for I won't do it."[20] His letter to a mother who had given five sons to the Union cause is a classic:

"I have been shown in the files of the War Department," wrote the President to Mrs. Lydia Bixby, a Boston widow, "a statement of the Adjutant General of Massachusetts that you are the mother of five sons who have died gloriously on the field of battle. I feel how weak and fruitless must be any word of mine which should attempt to beguile you from the grief of a loss so overwhelming. But I cannot refrain from tendering to you the consolation that may be found in the thanks of the republic they died to save. I pray that our heavenly Father may assuage the anguish of your bereavement and leave you only the cherished memory of the loved and lost, and the solemn pride that must be yours to have laid so costly a sacrifice upon the altar of freedom."[21]

With the Union armies victorious, the Stars and Stripes were raised again over Fort Sumter. It was Good Friday, April 14, 1865, in the second month of Lincoln's second term as President. That same evening, he and Mrs. Lincoln and a party of friends went to the theater where he was killed by an assassin's bullet.*

* One of Abraham Lincoln's last official actions, just before leaving for the theater, had been an act of clemency. Someone had placed in his hand a petition from a Confederate prisoner of war who had asked to be permitted to take the oath of allegiance and be set free. Lincoln had written across the petition. "Let it be done."[22]

In a story headlined, "The Great Crime—Abraham Lincoln's Place in History," the New York Herald referred to him as a *new* figure, "the type man of a new dynasty of nation-rulers," and proclaimed, "the triumph of the democratic principle . . . in our recent contest is an assurance that time has revolved this old earth on which we live into a new and perhaps happier—perhaps sadder—era."

His body was taken for burial to Springfield, Illinois, his old home. The whole nation mourned as the funeral train passed.

Shock-waves from Lincoln's murder were felt world-wide. Among personal letters of condolence received by Mrs. Lincoln was one from the widowed Queen Victoria. The British *Pall Mall Gazette* stated, "Lincoln was our best friend." French and German leaders and their people expressed their grief. In Scandinavian countries flags were at half mast. In the Orient, Japan, China and Siam framed messages of condolence. The Russian Leo Tolstoy, placing Lincoln among all the great heroes and statesmen of history, called him "the only real giant."

In thousands of commentaries, as analyzed by his biographer Carl Sandburg, Abraham Lincoln incarnated the two causes for which the war had been fought and won—emancipation and union.

Following the war, an almost explosive force of western expansion took place as homesteaders and railroad builders moved into the new territories. Now too, as a result flowing from the war, the United States would take its place among the nations counted as World Powers. And as a World Power, Carl Sandburg concludes, the expectation was that it would be "a voice of the teachings of Washington, Jefferson, Jackson—and Lincoln—speaking for republican government and democracy."

CONCLUSION

We hold these truths to be self-evident
That all men are created equal;
That they are endowed by their Creator
With certain unalienable Rights,
That among these are Life, Liberty
and the Pursuit of Happiness.
PREAMBLE TO THE DECLARATION OF INDEPENDENCE—1776[1]

IF the American Revolution had produced nothing but the Declaration of Independence it would have been worthwhile, states historian Samuel Eliot Morison. "The beauty and cogency of the Preamble, reaching back to remotest antiquity and forward to an indefinite future, have lifted the hearts of millions of men and will continue to do so," he concludes. "These words are more revolutionary than anything written by Robespierre, Marx or Lenin, more explosive than the atom, a continual challenge to ourselves as well as an inspiration to the oppressed of all the world."[2]

When the Constitutional Convention met in Philadelphia, the war was over, but this was far from being the case with the Revolution. "On the contrary," observed Dr. Benjamin Rush at the time, "only the first Act of the great drama is closed."[3]

From the beginning, the world has hopefully watched the unfolding of this "great drama." Men and women everywhere have looked to America's heritage as a trust for all mankind.

Where we have been faithful to this trust, the world has benefited. Where we have been faithless, the world has suffered.

As our third century opens, it is essential to recall that America's founders were thinking not only, or even primarily, of political and economic power. They envisioned "a new creation," a destiny to make a world happy, "to exhibit on the theatre of the Universe a character hitherto unknown."[4]

After his wars, George Washington's "first wish" was to see the whole world at peace—a true brotherhood of nations, with "each striving who should contribute most to the happiness of mankind."[5]

Such was the vision of the Founders. Today the world needs our food and our technology, but above all our faith. People want to know what America believes and whether or not we are going to live up to our beliefs.

John Adams, writing after the event, inquired what was meant by the American Revolution. The war was no part of it, he judged, only a result. The real revolution was in the minds of the people,[6] "the radical change in their principles, opinions, sentiments, affections"[7] which took place before a shot was fired at Lexington.

Since Lexington and Concord, revolutions have succeeded one another in America—social, industrial, scientific. Revolutionary advances of science are a commonplace of our time, and miracles of production have brought forth a society affluent beyond the dreams of earlier generations.

Today men span the stars, plumb the ocean depths, probe the secret of life itself. Man controls the atom. But can he control himself? We listen to "signals" from outer space. Do we listen to the inner Voice?*

A modern hurricane of change has transformed our environment, but it has not transformed us. Age-old antagonisms divide us, erode our national strength and threaten our standing in the world community.**

* "When man listens, God gives him ideas. And when man chooses to be governed by these ideas, he becomes a new type of man."[8]

FRANK N. D. BUCHMAN—1957

** Writing over 100 years ago, the British historian Macaulay pre-

Is our age destined to produce a new type of man and woman, with a revolutionary change in our motives to match the revolutionary march of our minds?

In this hope we can take heart from our history. "As they severally pursued their objects with ardor," relates an early historian of the first American revolutionaries, "a vast expansion of the human mind speedily followed." This new spirit displayed itself, he notes, in a variety of ways. "Men whose minds were warmed with the love of liberty," and whose abilities were heightened by daily exercise and a laudable ambition to serve their country, "spoke, wrote, and acted with an energy far surpassing all expectations,"[10] concluded this writer.

Americans owe a debt to outstanding leaders, but it must be remembered that this leadership was produced by a society of ordinary individuals who yet were capable of extraordinary achievements when inspired by imperative aims.* America was built upon the character of her people, and out of this "stronger structure of the spirit" is born the democracy we cherish.

It is the American people, then, to whom the world is looking for the next act in the "great drama." Will this call for a new plot and, above all, new characters?

"The American is a new man who acts upon new principles. . . ."

---

dicted to an American correspondent, "Your republic will be pillaged in the 20th Century . . . as Rome was in the 5th," not by barbarians, but "by her own citizens and the product of your own institutions."[9]

* "What Americans really want is not the promise of something for nothing, but a chance to give everything for something great."[11]

SENATOR HARRY S. TRUMAN—1943

EPILOGUE

"Annuit Coeptis"
(He looks with Favor on What Has Been Begun)[1]

"In the declaratory exordium which prefaces the Declaration of Rights, we see the solemn and majestic spectacle of a nation opening its commission, under the auspices of its Creator, to establish a Government; a scene so new . . . that the name of a revolution is diminutive of its character, and it rises into a regeneration of man."[2]

TOM PAINE—1793

APPENDIX

APPENDIX I

Money Talks

"I appoint Benjamin Franklin, John Adams and Thomas Jefferson a committee to prepare a device for a Great Seal of the United States," announced John Hancock, President of the Continental Congress, July 4, 1776, a few hours after the Declaration of Independence had been signed by the Delegates.

The "Device for a great Seal for the United States in Congress Assembled," was finally adopted in 1782. On the obverse, according to the *Remarks and Explanation*, the stripes of the escutcheon on the breast of the eagle "represent the Several States all joined in one solid compact entire" and the upper portion of the escutcheon "unites the whole and represents Congress." The motto, 'E Pluribus Unum' (one out of many) "alludes to this union . . . The olive branch and arrows denote the power of peace and war . . . The Constellation denotes a new State taking its place among other sovereign powers." On the reverse, the pyramid "signifies Strength and Duration"; the eye over it and the motto, 'Annuit Coeptis'—(He has favored our undertakings) "allude to the many signal interpositions of providence in favor of the American Cause." The date 1776 and the words 'Novus Ordo Seclorum' (a new order of the ages) "signify the beginning of the new American Aera (*sic*) which commences from that date."

The seal is in charge of the Secretary of State, and is affixed to Presidential proclamations, ratification of treaties, commissions of Cabinet Members, U.S. Ambassadors, ministers and Foreign Service Officers, and certain other documents after they have been signed by the President.

During the F. D. Roosevelt Administration, the dollar bill was redesigned and the reverse of the Great Seal added to it.

COINAGE

"There has indeed been an intention to strike copper coin. . . . Instead of repeating continually upon every halfpenny the dull story that everybody knows . . . that George III is King of Great Britain . . . etc. to put on one side, some important proverb of Solomon, some pious moral, prudential or economical precept, the frequent inculcation of which, by seeing it every time one receives a piece of money, might make an impression on the mind, especially of young persons, and tend to regulate the conduct, such as, on some, 'The fear of the Lord is the beginning of wisdom.' "

BENJAMIN FRANKLIN, *letter to Edward Bridgen*
—October 2, 1779[1]

In November, 1861, Salmon P. Chase, Secretary of the Treasury and one of President Lincoln's ablest Cabinet Ministers, dispatched a note to the Director of the Mint in Philadelphia. "No nation can be strong except in the strength of God," wrote the Secretary, "or safe except in His defense. The trust of our people in God should be declared on our national coins.

"You will cause a device to be prepared without unnecessary delay with a motto expressing in the fewest and tersest words possible this national recognition."

It was in 1864 that the motto "In God We Trust" first appeared and since then many issues of all our coins have borne this simple affirmation of a nation's faith.

(Note) Salmon P. Chase became Chief Justice of the United States Supreme Court, 1864–1873. The Chase National Bank, chartered in 1877, was named in honor of him.

The Mayflower Compact
November 11, 1620

"In ye name of God, Amen. We whose names are under-written, the loyall subjects of our dread soveraigne Lord, King James, by ye grace of God, of Great Britaine, France, and Ireland king, defender of ye faith, &c. haveing under-taken, for ye glorie of God, and advancemente of ye Chris-tian faith, and honour of our king & countrie, a voyage to plant ye first colonie in ye Northerne parts of Virginia, doe by these presents solemnly & mutually in ye presence of God, and one of another, covenant & combine ourselves togeather into a civill body politick, for our better ordering & preservation & furtherance of ye ends aforesaid; and by vertue hereof to enacte, constitute, and frame such just & equal lawes, ordinances, acts, constitutions, & offices, from time to time, as shall be thought most meete & convenient for ye generall good of ye Colonie, unto which we promise all due submission and obedience. In witness whereof we have hereunder subscribed our names at Cap-Codd ye 11 of November, in ye year of ye raigne of our soveraigne lord, King James, of England, France & Ireland ye eighteenth, and of Scotland ye fiftie fourth. Ano: Dom. 1620."

* * *

John Quincy Adams, in 1802, observed of The Mayflower Compact: "This is perhaps the only instance in human history of that positive, original social compact which speculative philosophers have imagined as the only legiti-mate source of government. Here was a unanimous and personal assent by all the individuals of the community to the association, *by which they became a nation.* The settlers of all the former European colonies had contented them-selves with the powers conferred upon them by their respec-tive charters, without looking beyond the seal of the royal

parchment for the measure of their rights and the rule of
their duties. The founders of Plymouth had been impelled
by the peculiarities of their situation to examine the subject
with deeper and more comprehensive research."

APPENDIX III

GEORGE WHITEFIELD—A FARMER'S ACCOUNT

· " 'One morning all on a suding about 8 or 9 o'clock came
a messinger and said Mr. whitfield preached at hartford
and weathersfield yesterday and is to preach at middletown
this morning (October 23, 1740) at 10 o'clock i was in my
field at work i dropt my tool that i had in my hand and
run home and run thru the house and bad my wife get
ready quick to goo and hear mr whitfield preach at middletown and run to my pasture for my hors with all my might
fearing i should be late to hear him i brought my hors home
and soon mounted and took my wife up and went forward
as fast as i thought the hors could bear, and when my hors
began to be out of breath i would get down and put my
wife on ye saddel and bid her ride as fast as she could and
not stop or slak for me except i bad her and so I would
run until i was almost out of breth and then mount my hors
again and so I did several times to favour my hors we im-
proved every moment to get along as if we were fleeing for
our lives all this while fearing we should be too late to
hear ye sermon for we had twelve miles to ride dubble in
littel more than an hour. . . .'

"As they drew near Middletown he observed a fog, which
he thought was arising from the river and heard a sound
like low rumbling thunder, but soon he discovered that
what he thought was thunder, 'was ye rumbling of horses
feet coming down ye road' and the fog 'was a Cloud of dust
made by running horses feet.' When they came near to the
main road they could seen man and horses 'slipping along
in ye Cloud like shadows' and when they drew nearer 'it

was like a stedy stream of horses and their riders scarcely a horse more than his length behind another all of a lather' . . . while 'every hors seemed to go with all his might to carry his rider to hear ye news from heaven for the saving of their souls it made me trembel to see ye sight.'

"Arriving in Middletown, he found a great multitude of some three or four thousand had assembled. The river bank was black with people and horses, while 'fery boats (were) running swift forward and backward bringing over loads of people ye ores roed nimble and quick every thing men horses and boats all seamed to be struglin for life.' He saw Mr. Whitefield arrive and ascend 'ye Scaffil' and Whitefield 'looked almost angellical a young slim slender youth' . . . 'with bold countenance.' All this 'solumnized' his mind and put him in 'a trembling fear' . . . for 'he looked as if he was Cloathed with authority from yet great god and a sweet collome Solumnity sat upon his brow and my hearing him preach gave me a heart wound by God's blessing . . . my old foundation was broken up & i saw that my righteousness would not save me. . . .' "

From a MS letter in Yale University[2]

George Whitefield and Benjamin Franklin

"The multitudes of all sects and denominations that attended (Whitefield's) sermons were enormous, and it was matter of speculation to me, who was one of the number, to observe the extraordinary influence of his oratory upon his hearers, and how much they admired and respected him, notwithstanding his common abuse of them, by assuring them that they were half beasts and half devils. It was wonderful to see the change soon made in half our inhabitants. From being thoughtless or indifferent about religion, it seems as if all the world were growing religious, so that one could not walk thro' the town in an evening without hearing psalms sung in different families of every street."

Benjamin Franklin, Autobiography

"I am glad that you have frequent opportunities of preaching among the great," Franklin wrote to Whitefield, July 6, 1749, "If you can gain them to a good and exemplary life, wonderful changes will follow in the manners of the lower ranks; for ad exemplum regis, etc. On this principle, Confucius, the famous eastern reformer, proceeded. When he saw his country sunk in vice and wickedness of all kinds triumphant, he applied himself first to the grandees; and having by his doctrine, won them to the cause of virtue, the commons followed in multitudes. The mode has a wonderful influence on mankind; and there are numbers, who, perhaps, fear less the being in hell than out of fashion. Our more western reformation began with the ignorant mob; and, when numbers of them were gained, interest and party-views drew in the wise and great. Where both methods can be used, reformations are likely to be more speedy." Franklin concludes piously, "Oh that some methods could be found to make them lasting! He who discovers that, will, in my opinion, deserve more, ten thousand times, than the inventor of the longitude. . . .

"My wife and family join in the most cordial salutations to you and good Mrs. Whitefield. . . ."

That Whitefield exerted a tactful pressure on his friend is suggested by a letter from London in 1752:

"I find that you grow more and more famous in the learned world," he wrote to Franklin, "As you have made a pretty considerable progress in the mysteries of electricity I would now humbly recommend to your diligent unprejudiced pursuit and study the mysteries of the New Birth. It is a most important, interesting study, and when mastered, will richly answer and repay for all your pains . . . You will excuse this freedom. I must have 'aliquid Christi' (Something of Christ) in all my letters."

In what was probably the last letter George Whitefield wrote to Benjamin Franklin he closed with the words: "ere long . . . angels shall summon us to attend on the funeral of time, and we shall see eternity rising out of its ashes.

That you and I may be in the happy number of those
who . . . shall cry, 'Amen! Hallelujah!' is the hearty prayer
of, my dear Doctor, yours, etc. George Whitefield."

APPENDIX IV

"The real wonder is that so many difficulties should
have been . . . surmounted with an unanimity almost as
unprecedented, as it must have been unexpected. . . . It
is impossible, for the man of pious reflection, not to perceive in it a finger of that Almighty Hand, which has been
so frequently and signally extended to our relief in the
critical stages of the revolution."

JAMES MADISON. *The Federalist*[3]

THE CONSTITUTION OF THE UNITED STATES

PREAMBLE

We the people of the United States, in order to form a
more perfect union, establish justice, ensure domestic tran-
quility, provide for the common defense, promote the general welfare, and secure the blessings of liberty to ourselves
and our posterity, do ordain and establish this Constitution
for the United States of America.

AMENDMENTS I THROUGH X

(The Bill of Rights)

Article I

Congress shall make no law respecting an establishment
of religion, or prohibiting the free exercise thereof; or
abridging the freedom of speech, or of the press; or the
right of the people peaceably to assemble, and to petition
the Government for a redress of grievances.

Article II

A well regulated Militia, being necessary to the security of a free State, the right of the people to keep and bear Arms, shall not be infringed.

Article III

No Soldier shall, in time of peace, be quartered in any house, without the consent of the Owner, nor in time of war, but in a manner to be prescribed by law.

Article IV

The right of the people to be secure in their persons, houses, papers, and effects, against unreasonable searches and seizures, shall not be violated, and no warrants shall issue, but upon probable cause, supported by Oath of affirmation, and particularly describing the place to be searched, and the person or things to be seized.

Article V

No Person shall be held to answer for a capital, or otherwise infamous crime, unless on a presentment of indictment of a Grand Jury, except in cases arising in the land or naval forces, or in the Militia, when in actual service in time of War or public danger; nor shall any person be subject for the same offence to be twice put in jeopardy of life or limb; nor shall be compelled in any criminal case to be a witness against himself, nor be deprived of life, liberty, or property, without due process of law; nor shall private property be taken for public use, without just compensation.

Article VI

In all criminal prosecutions the accused shall enjoy the right to a speedy and public trial, by an impartial jury of the State and district wherein the crime shall have been committed, which district shall have been previously ascertained by law, and to be informed of the nature and cause of the accusation; to be confronted with the witnesses against him; to have compulsory process for obtaining witnesses in his favor, and to have the Assistance of Counsel for his defence.

Article VII

In Suits at common law, where the value in controversy shall exceed twenty dollars, the right of trial by jury shall be preserved, and no fact tried by a jury shall be otherwise re-examined in any Court of the United States, than according to the rules of the common law.

Article VIII

Excessive bail shall not be required, nor excessive fines imposed, nor cruel and unusual punishments inflicted.

Article IX

The enumeration in the Constitution, of certain rights shall not be construed to deny or disparage others retained by the people.

Article X

The powers not delegated to the United States by the Constitution, nor prohibited by it to the States, are reserved to the States respectively, or to the people.

APPENDIX V

JOHN QUINCY ADAMS

John Quincy Adams (1767–1848) was born the year after the repeal of the Stamp Act; he died thirteen years before the outbreak of the Civil War. He was the last of the "revolutionary generation" of United States Chief Executives.

There were close personal bonds between these men. John Adams and Thomas Jefferson had carried national burdens with Washington and held him in boundless esteem and affection. James Madison and James Monroe, Virginia neighbors of Jefferson, were friends as well and political colleagues. The Adams-Jefferson friendship survived many vicissitudes, and terminated only in their deaths—within a few hours of each other—upon the 50th Anniversary of the signing of the Declaration of Independence.

John Quincy Adams concluded this extraordinary succession. Like his father, he had been a Federalist but, as Senator, he voted with the Republicans on the question of the Louisiana Purchase and, in the same year, attended the Republican caucus that nominated Madison for the Presidency.

By inheritance and training, John Quincy Adams was singularly qualified for national leadership. Before he was fourteen, he had twice accompanied his father to Europe. He studied in Paris and at Leyden University; went to Russia with Francis Dana, returned to Paris and joined his father as "secretary" to the American Commissioners in the peace negotiations with Britain. Returning to Massachusetts, he graduated from Harvard College in 1787 and practiced law in Boston. In 1794, he was sent as American Minister to The Hague but, when his father was elected President, he was transferred to Berlin where he negotiated a commerce treaty with Prussia. After Jefferson's election as President, the elder Adams recalled his son who returned home in 1801. The following year, he was called to the Massachusetts Senate and, in 1803, went to Washington as a member of the Senate of the United States. There, his support of the Administration cost him his seat. He joined the Harvard faculty as Professor of oratory and rhetoric. Three years later, President Madison appointed him United States Minister to Russia. He took part in negotiations with Britain which resulted in the Treaty of Ghent and concluded the War of 1812. Adams was in Paris to witness the return of Napoleon from Elba, then went to

London in the post of United States Minister to Great Britain, like his father before him (and his son after him). He returned to the United States in 1817 to become Secretary of State in President James Monroe's Cabinet.

As Secretary of State, Adams was mainly responsible for the United States' acquisition of Florida and promulgation of the "Monroe Doctrine." He was elected President in 1825 and served one term. Defeated for re-election by Andrew Jackson, he retired to private life. A year later, he ran for Congress, spurning the suggestion that a lower office might "degrade" the ex-President. He was elected to the House where he served for seventeen years.

Although not an "abolitionist," John Quincy Adams became a leader in the developing anti-slavery movement which had begun with the publication of *The Liberator* by William Lloyd Garrison in 1831. He saw in the Missouri Compromise,* ". . . a mere preamble—a title-page to a great, tragic volume," and for thirteen years he led the fight in Congress against the "gag-rules" by which pro-slavery forces had blocked action by their opponents. In 1844, Adams was finally successful in getting the offending measures repealed.

On February 21, 1848, he suffered a heart attack on the floor of the Chamber and died two days later.

APPENDIX VI

THE VIRGINIA STATUTE OF RELIGIOUS LIBERTY

October, 1785
An Act for establishing Religious Freedom.

I) Whereas Almighty God hath created the mind free; that all attempts to influence it by temporal punishments or burthens, or by civil incapacitations, . . . are a departure from the plan of the Holy author of our religion, who being Lord both of body and mind, yet chose not to propagate

* Acts of Congress in 1820 whereby Missouri was admitted to the Union as a 'slave State' and Maine as a 'free State,' and slavery was prohibited in the United States territory north of Latitude 36°30'.

it by coercions on either . . . that to compel a man to furnish contributions of money for the propagation of opinions which he disbelieves, is sinful and tyrannical; . . . that our civil rights have no dependence on our religious opinions . . . that therefore the proscribing any citizen as unworthy of public confidence . . . unless he profess or renounce this or that religious opinion, is depriving him injuriously of those privileges and advantages to which in common with his fellow-citizens he has a natural right . . . that to suffer the civil magistrate to intrude his powers into the field of opinion, and to restrain the profession or propagation of principles on supposition of their ill tendency, is a dangerous fallacy, which at once destroys all religious liberty . . . that it is time enough for the rightful purposes of civil government, for its officers to interfere when principles break out into overt acts against peace and good order; and finally, that truth is great and will prevail if left to herself, that she is the proper and sufficient antagonist to error, and has nothing to fear from the conflict, unless by human interposition disarmed of her natural weapons, free argument and debate, errors ceasing to be dangerous when it is permitted freely to contradict them.

II) Be it enacted by the General Assembly, that no man shall be compelled to frequent or support any religious worship, place or ministry whatsoever, nor shall be enforced, restrained, molested, or burthened in his body or goods, nor shall otherwise suffer on account of his religious opinions or belief; but that all men shall be free to profess, and by argument to maintain their opinion in matters of religion, and that the same shall in no wise diminish, enlarge, or affect their civil capacities.

III) And though we well know that this Assembly, elected by the people . . . have no power to restrain the acts of succeeding Assemblies, . . . yet as we are free to declare, and do declare, that the rights hereby asserted are of the natural rights of mankind, and that if any Act hereafter be passed to repeal the present, or to narrow its operation, such Act will be an infringement of natural rights.

APPENDIX VII

THE NORTHWEST ORDINANCE

July 13, 1787

(An Ordinance for the government of the Territory of
the United States northwest of the River Ohio.)

The "Western Problem" posed by the unsettled parts of
the North American Continent, reached back to the earliest
times of European settlement. It involved competing interests of European Powers as well as relationships between
Indians and frontiersmen, control and regulation of the fur
trade, acquisition and disposal of public lands, and the
degree of self-government to be granted the new settlements, and their relations with the older colonies, the Empire and, eventually, the United States of America.

The Treaty of Paris in 1763 eliminated French claims
(except New Orleans) and divided the West by the Mississippi River between the Spanish and British Empires. The
remaining problems persisted and were shortly to crowd in
upon the new United States Government.

While the Constitutional Convention in Philadelphia was
debating a plan to "revise" the Articles of Confederation,
the Continental Congress, meeting in New York passed
one of their last and most significant measures. "The Northwest Ordinance, based largely on an earlier report by Jefferson, belongs to the first rank of American constitutional
documents," states Morison. "Noteworthy alike are the bill
of rights, the provisions for representative government, for
future statehood, and for the exclusion of slavery. It provided the United States with a colonial system, on the basis
of equal rights between new and old communities. It was
the most important single step toward the solution of the
Western problem. . . ."[4]

The Northwest Ordinance still stands superior to all
constitutions and laws subsequently adopted by the five

states—Ohio, Indiana, Illinois, Michigan and Wisconsin—which have been created out of the Northwest Territory.

APPENDIX VIII

Speech by Benjamin Franklin at the Constitutional Convention—Philadelphia, 1787

It was to have been the privilege of Benjamin Franklin to nominate George Washington as President of the Constitutional Convention which convened in Philadelphia May 25, 1787. Unluckily, a drenching rain that day kept the ailing Dr. Franklin housebound. However, when regular sessions began a few days later, he was in attendance and continued with remarkable regularity during the sixteen hot summer weeks of the Convention.

Franklin stated the true purpose of such deliberative bodies: "We are sent to consult not contend with each other," he maintained, "and declarations of a fixed opinion, and determined resolution never to change it, neither enlighten nor convince us . . . Harmony and union are extremely necessary to give weight to our councils and render them effectual in promoting and securing the common good."

In support of his motion to employ a chaplain and open the sessions with prayer, Franklin addressed the Convention:

"Mr. President: The small progress we have made after four or five weeks close attendance and continual reasonings with each other—our different sentiments on almost every question, several of the last producing as many noes as ayes, is methinks a melancholy proof of the imperfection of the human understanding. We indeed seem to feel our own want of political wisdom, since we have been running about in search of it. We have gone back to ancient history for models of government, and examined the different forms of those republics which, having been formed with the seeds of their own dissolution, no longer exist. And we have viewed modern states all around Europe, but find none of their Constitutions suitable to our circumstances.

"In this situation of this Assembly, groping as it were in the dark to find political truth, and scarce able to distinguish it when presented us, how has it happened, Sir, that we have not hitherto once thought of humbly applying to the Father of Lights to illumine our understanding? In the beginning of the contest with Great Britain, when we were sensible of danger we had daily prayer in this room for the divine protection. Our prayers, Sir, were heard, and they were graciously answered. All of us who were engaged in the struggle must have observed frequent instances of a superintending Providence in our favor. To that kind Providence we owe this happy opportunity of consulting in peace on the means of establishing our future national felicity. And have we now forgotten that powerful Friend? Or do we imagine that we no longer need His assistance?

"I have lived, Sir, a long time, and the longer I live, the more convincing proofs I see of this truth—that God governs in the affairs of men. And if a sparrow cannot fall to the ground without His notice, is it probable that an empire can rise without His aid? We have been assured, Sir, in the sacred writings, that 'except the Lord build the house they labor in vain that build it.' I firmly believe this, and I also believe that without His concurring aid we shall succeed in this political building no better than the builders of Babel. We shall be divided by our little partial local interests, our projects will be confounded, and we ourselves shall become a reproach and by-word to future ages. And what is worse, mankind may hereafter from this unfortunate instance, despair of establishing governments by human wisdom and leave it to chance, war, and conquest."

By the President of the United States of America

A PROCLAMATION

Whereas the Senate of the United States, devoutly recognizing the supreme authority and just government of Almighty God in all the affairs of men and nations, has by a resolution requested the President to designate and set apart a day for national prayer and humiliation; and

Whereas it is the duty of nations as well as of men to own their dependence upon the overruling power of God, to confess their sins and transgressions in humble sorrow, yet with assured hope that genuine repentence will lead to mercy and pardon, and to recognize the sublime truth, announced in the Holy Scriptures and proven by all history, that those nations only are blessed whose God is the Lord;

And, insomuch as we know that by His divine law nations, like individuals, are subjected to punishments and chastisements in this world, may we not justly fear that the awful calamity of civil war which now desolates the land may be but a punishment inflicted upon us for our presumptuous sins, to the needful end of our national reformation as a whole people? We have been the recipients of the choicest bounties of Heaven; we have grown in numbers, wealth, and power as no other nation has ever grown. But we have forgotten God. We have forgotten the gracious hand which preserved us in peace and multiplied and enriched and strengthened us, and we have vainly imagined, in the deceitfulness of our hearts, that all these blessings were produced by some superior wisdom and virtue of our own. Intoxicated with unbroken success, we have become too self-sufficient to feel the necessity of redeeming and preserving grace, too proud to pray to the God that made us.

It behooves us, then, to humble ourselves before the offended Power, to confess our national sins, and to pray for clemency and forgiveness.

Now, therefore, in compliance with the request, and fully concurring in the view of the Senate, I do by this my proclamation designate and set apart Thursday, the 30th day of April, 1863, as a day of national humiliation, fasting, and prayer. And I do hereby request all the people to abstain on that day from their ordinary secular pursuits, and to unite at their several places of public worship and their respective homes in keeping the day holy to the Lord and devoted to the humble discharge of the religious duties proper to that solemn occasion.

All this being done in sincerity and truth, let us then rest humble in the hope authorized by the divine teachings that the united cry of the nation will be heard on high and answered with blessings no less than the pardon of our national sins and the restoration of our now divided and suffering country to its former happy condition of unity and peace.

In witness whereof I have hereunto set my hand and caused the seal of the United States to be affixed.

(SEAL)

Done at the City of Washington, this 30th day of March, A.D. 1863, and of the Independence of the United States the eighty-seventh.

ABRAHAM LINCOLN

By the President:

WILLIAM H. SEWARD, *Secretary of State*

ABRAHAM LINCOLN
THE GETTYSBURG ADDRESS—NOV. 19, 1863

At about the mid-point of the war, November, 1863, Lincoln accepted an invitation to take part in the dedication of a National Soldiers' Cemetery at Gettysburg, Pennsylvania, and make "a few appropriate remarks." Featured orator of the day was the distinguished Massachusetts statesman, diplomat and educator, Edward Everett. Following him, Lincoln made a brief address. In this he took the occasion to clarify the principles in defense of which the soldiers had died, and for which the Union would continue to fight. The speech had a mixed reception from the press. Everett wrote to Lincoln the following day: "I should be glad if I could flatter myself that I came as close to the central idea of the occasion in two hours as you did in two minutes."

Probably no one has ever come closer to America's "central idea" than Lincoln in the Gettysburg Address.

* * *

Fourscore and seven years ago, our fathers brought forth upon this continent a new nation, conceived in liberty and dedicated to the proposition that all men are created equal.

Now we are engaged in a great civil war, testing whether that nation—or any nation, so conceived and so dedicated —can long endure.

We are met on a great battle-field of that war. We have come to dedicate a portion of it as the final resting place of those who have given their lives that that nation might live.

It is altogether fitting and proper that we should do this.

But, in a larger sense, we cannot dedicate—we cannot consecrate—we cannot hallow—this ground. The brave men, living and dead, who struggled here, have consecrated it, far above our poor power to add or to detract.

The world will little note, nor long remember what we say here, but it can never forget what they did here.

It is for us, the living, rather, to be dedicated here to the unfinished work which they have thus far so nobly carried on. It is rather for us to be here dedicated to the great task remaining before us—that from these honored dead we take increased devotion to that cause for which they here gave the last full measure of devotion—that we here highly resolve that these dead shall not have died in vain—that this nation, under God, shall have a new birth of freedom, and that government of the people, by the people, for the people, shall not perish from the earth.

CHRONOLOGY

America	England	World
1492 Columbus' first voyage	1509 Accession of Henry VIII	1517 Martin Luther begins the Reformation
1497–98 John Cabot's voyages		1519 Charles V crowned Holy Roman Emperor
		1519–21 Magellan circumnavigates the globe
1523–24 Giovanni da Verrazano's voyage	1526 First English Bible	1534 Ignatius Loyola founds the Jesuit Order
1534–41 Jacques Cartier's voyages		1545 Council of Trent
	1547 Accession of Edward VI	
	1553 Accession of Mary	
	1558 Accession of Elizabeth I	Emperor Charles V abdicates
	1564 Birth of Shakespeare	

America	England	World
		1572 Massacre of St. Bartholomew's Eve
1576–78 Martin Frobisher's voyages		
1585 "Lost Colony" of Roanoke		
	1588 British Fleet defeats Spanish Armada	
	1603 James VI of Scotland becomes James I of England	
1603–35 Samuel de Champlain's voyages to eastern Canada	1605 Guy Fawkes and the "Gunpowder Plot"	
1607 Founding of Jamestown		
1608–11 Henry Hudson's voyages		
1608 Founding of Quebec		
		1618–48 Thirty Years War
1619 Virginia House of Burgesses, first representative government		
First Negro slaves imported into Virginia		
1620 Founding of Plymouth Colony Mayflower Compact		
1624 Founding of New Amsterdam by the Dutch	1625 Accession of Charles I	

America	England	World
1630 Founding of Massachusetts Bay Colony		
1634 Maryland settled		
1635 Connecticut settled		
1636 Rhode Island settled Harvard College founded		
1639 "Fundamental Orders" of Connecticut, first written constitution		
1639 Act of Toleration, Maryland		
	1642–59 Civil Wars	
		1648 Peace of Westphalia ends Thirty Years War
	1649 Trial and execution of Charles I Establishment of Commonwealth under Oliver Cromwell	
	1660 Restoration of Charles II	
1663 Founding of Carolina		
1664 Delaware and New Jersey founded New York established	1665 Great Plague of London	

America	England	World
	1666 Great Fire of London	
1683 Penn's Treaty with the Indians		1683 Turks besiege Vienna
	1688 James II deposed "The Glorious Revolution"	
1689 King William's War, first war with the French and Indians	1689-97 "King William's War"	1689-1725 Reign of Peter the Great of Russia
1693 William and Mary College founded		1694 Voltaire born
1701 Yale College founded	1701 War of the Spanish Succession	
1702 "Queen Anne's War"	1702 Accession of Queen Anne	
1703 Jonathan Edwards born		
1704 The Deerfield Massacre	1704 Battle of Blenheim won by Duke of Marlborough	
1706 Benjamin Franklin born		1707 Death of Aurangzeb, breakup of Mogul Empire in India
		1709 Battle of Poltara Brother Junipero Serra born
1713 Treaty of Utrecht ends Queen Anne's War	1714 Accession of George I of Hanover	

World

1718 Spanish found San Antonio
French found New Orleans

1721 Johann Sebastian Bach's
"Brandenburg Concertos"

1724 Yung Cheng expels
Christian missionaries from China

1728 Bering discovers the
Bering Straits

England

1715 Attempt to restore the
Stuarts, "The Old Pretender"

1721 Sir Robert Walpole becomes
Prime Minister of England.
His policy of "benign neglect"
toward colonies prevails until 1760

1726 Accession of George II

1739 "War of Jenkin's Ear"

America

1726 Beginning of "The Great
Awakening"

1729 North Carolina becomes
separate colony

1732 George Washington born

1733 Georgia founded

1735 Peter Zenger's acquittal establishes
freedom of the press

1735 Thomas Jefferson born

1736 John Wesley begins American
preaching tour

World

1740–86 Frederick the Great, King of Prussia

1740–80 Maria Theresa of Austria

1749 Goethe born

1757 Battle of Plassey won by Clive of India
Lafayette born
Tongs established in China

1762–96 Catherine the Great, Empress of Russia

England

1742 Handel's "Messiah"

1745 "The '45," Bonnie Prince Charlie, the "Young Pretender" British take Louisbourg from the French

1757 Ministry of William Pitt, the elder

1760 Accession of George III

America

1741 Jonathan Edwards' "Sinners in the Hands of an Angry God"

1753 George Washington receives a commission in the Virginia Militia

1754–63 French & Indian War

1755 Defeat of General Braddock
Alexander Hamilton born

1759 General Wolfe takes Quebec from the French

1763 Peace of Paris ends French & Indian War
Pontiac's Rebellion

1764 Revenue Act

America	England	World
1765 Stamp Act	1765 Watts' improved steam engine	1765 Clive establishes British administration in India
1766 Stamp Act repealed	Blackstone's "Commentaries on the Laws of England"	
1769 Spain establishes first mission in California		
1770 "Boston Massacre"	1770 Lord North becomes Prime Minister	
1772 First Committees of Correspondence founded		1772 First partition of Poland by Russia, Prussia and Austria
1773 Boston Tea Party		1773 Jesuits suppressed by Pope Clement XIV
		Warren Hastings appointed Governor-General of India
1774 First Continental Congress		1774 Accession of Louis XVI, King of France (1774–93)
1775–83 War of American Independence		
1776 Declaration of Independence	1776 City of London remonstrates against American War	
Tom Paine's "Common Sense"	Adam Smith's "Wealth of Nations"	
1777 Battle of Saratoga		
Continental Army winters at Valley Forge		

America	England	World
1778 French Alliance		
	1780 Gordon riots in London	
1781 Articles of Confederation ratified Surrender of Cornwallis at Yorktown		1781 Kant's "Critique of Pure Reason"
1783 Peace of Versailles ends Revolutionary War		1783 Simon Bolivar born in Caracas First balloon ascent in Paris
1786 Virginia adopts Jefferson's Statute for Religious Freedom Virginia cedes western lands to Congress Shay's Rebellion in Massachusetts		
1787 Constitutional Convention Northwest Ordinance		
1788 Ratification of the Constitution		
1789 George Washington inaugurated President (1789–97)		1789 Fall of the Bastille
1790 Benjamin Franklin dies First national census		
1791 Bill of Rights	1791 John Wesley dies	
		1792 First French Republic (1792–1804)

America	England	World
		1793 Louis XVI guillotined
		Reign of Terror
		Establishment of Consulate
		The French Republic declares war on England
1794 Jay's Treaty with England		1794 Kosciuszko leads a revolt in Poland
1795 Pinckney's Treaty with Spain		
Ohio lands ceded by Indians after Battle of Fallen Timbers		
1796 Washington's Farewell Address		
1797 John Adams inaugurated President (1797–1801)		
	1798 Malthus' "An Essay on the Principles of Population"	
1799 Death of George Washington		
1800 Washington becomes new capital city		
1801 Thomas Jefferson inaugurated President (1801–1809)		
1803 Louisiana Purchase		

America	England	World
		1804 Napoleon proclaimed emperor of France (1804–14)
	1805 Nelson defeats French at Trafalgar	
	1807 Slave trade abolished throughout the British Empire	
1808 Importation of slaves abolished		
1809 James Madison inaugurated President (1809–17)		1810 Mexican War for Independence
	1811 George III declared insane Regency established	1812 Napoleon invades Russia
1812–15 War with England		
1814 Peace of Ghent ends War		
1815 Battle of New Orleans		1815 Battle of Waterloo Congress of Vienna
		1816 Argentine provinces declared independent at Tucuman
1817 James Monroe inaugurated President (1817–25) Construction begun on the Erie Canal		
1819 Florida acquired by treaty with Spain		

America	England	World
1820 Missouri Compromise	1820 Accession of George IV (1820–30)	1821 Mexico wins independence
		1822 Pedro I crowned Emperor of Brazil Ecuador joins Colombia and Venezuela in Republic of Gran Colombia O'Higgins declares Chile independent at Talca
1823 Monroe Doctrine		1823 "United Provinces of Central America" proclaimed at Guatemala City
1824 Lafayette visits United States		
1825 John Quincy Adams inaugurated President (1825–29)		1825 Bolivia proclaims independence at La Paz Portugal recognizes independence of Brazil
1826 Death of Thomas Jefferson and John Adams		1826 Last Spanish Garrison surrenders at Callao, Peru

BIBLIOGRAPHY

So many books have been written on almost every aspect of early American history that the modern reader finds it difficult to choose between them. Moreover, we have little time to read and so (in Isaac Newton's phrase), "the great ocean of truth" lies all undiscovered before us. Yet we can expect exciting discoveries in books. Nuggets of wisdom, experience and faith lie ready to be mined out of our past. As an introduction to our history, there can be no substitute, of course, for the actual writings of the men and women who took part in the building of America. The autobiographies of Benjamin Franklin, Thomas Jefferson and the Adamses with their diaries, letters and speeches bring to life, as nothing else can, the character and personalities of these great figures. Selections from their works by editors, such as Adrienne Koch and William Peden, are helpful to the general reader. Early histories by Governor William Bradford, Benjamin Trumbull and David Ramsey, as well as authoritative biographies—Douglas Southall Freeman's "George Washington," for example, and Carl Sandburg's "Lincoln"—repay careful study. Many readers find pleasure and profit in historical narratives, among which "Miracle at Philadelphia" by Catherine Drinker Bowen and "Those Who Love" by Irving Stone come readily to mind.

The following pages list suggested works for general reading and research. Most of these books, as well as reprints of early works, can be found in major libraries. Librarians can recommend additional reading from the wealth of American historical material available today.

Adams, Charles Francis, ed. *The Familiar Letters of John Adams and His Wife, Abigail Adams.* Cambridge, Mass.: Riverside Press, 1876.

Adams, Charles Francis, ed. *The Works of John Adams.* 10 vols. Boston: Little, Brown & Co., 1850–1856.

Adams, James Truslow. *The American.* New York: Charles Scribner's Sons, 1943.

Ahlstrom, Sydney E. *A Religious History of the American People.* New Haven and London: Yale University Press, 1973.

Alexander, Archibald. *Biographical Sketches of the Founder and Principal Alumni of the Log College.* Princeton: J. T. Robinson, 1846.

Allison, John Murray. *Adams and Jefferson, The Story of a Friendship.* Norman: University of Oklahoma Press, 1966.

Andrews, Charles M. *The Colonial Period of American History.* Vol. II, "The Settlements." New Haven: Yale University Press, 1936.

Andrews, M. P. *The Soul of a Nation.* New York: Charles Scribner's Sons, 1943.

Backus, Isaac. *A History of New England.* 2 vols. Vol. I, Boston: E. Draper, 1777; Vol. II, Providence: J. Carter, 1784.

Bailyn, Bernard. *The Ideological Origins of the American Revolution.* Cambridge, Mass.: The Belknap Press of Harvard University Press, 1967.

Baldwin, Alice Mary. *The New England Clergy and the American Revolution.* Durham, N.C.: Duke University Press, 1928.

Bancroft, George. *History of the Colonization of the United States.* Boston: Little, Brown & Co., 1840.

Barton, William E. *Congregational Creeds and Covenants.* Chicago: Advance Publishing Co., 1917.

Basler, Roy Prentice. *Abraham Lincoln; His Speeches and Writings.* Cleveland and New York: World Publishing Co., 1946.

Basler, Roy Prentice. *The Collected Works of Abraham Lincoln.* New Brunswick, N.J.: Rutgers University Press, 1953.

Becker, Carl L. *The Declaration of Independence, A Study in the History of Political Ideas.* New York: Vintage Books, Random House, Inc., 1942.

Benjamin Franklin on Religion. Philadelphia: The Franklin Institute, 1938.

Beverly, Robert. *The History and Present State of Virginia, 1705.* Chapel Hill: University of North Carolina Press, 1947.

Belden, Albert D. *George Whitefield—The Awakener.* London: S. Low, Marston & Co., 1930.

Boorstin, Daniel J. *The Americans.* 3 vols. New York: Random House, 1958.

Borgeand, Charles. *The Rise of Modern Democracy in England and New England.* New York: Charles Scribner's Sons, 1894.

Bowen, Catherine Drinker. *John Adams and the American Revolution.* Boston: Little, Brown & Co., 1950.

Bowen, Catherine Drinker. *Miracle at Philadelphia.* Boston: Little, Brown & Co., 1966.

Bowers, Claude G. *Jefferson and Hamilton, The Struggle for Democracy in America.* Boston and New York, Houghton Mifflin Co., 1925.

Bowers, Claude G. *The Young Jefferson, 1743–1789.* Boston and New York: Houghton Mifflin Co., 1945.

Boyd, Julian P., ed. *The Papers of Thomas Jefferson.* Princeton: Princeton University Press, 1953. Of this series, 19 volumes have so far been published.

Bradford, William. *Of Plymouth Plantation.* Samuel Eliot Morison, ed. New York: Knopf, 1952.

Bridenbaugh, Carl and Jessica. *Rebels and Gentlemen; Philadelphia in the Age of Franklin.* New York: Reynal & Hitchcock, 1942.

Brodhead, John Romeyn. *History of the State of New York.* New York: Harper & Brothers, 1853.

Brown, L. F. *Political Activities of the Baptists and Fifth Monarchy Men in England during the Interregnum.* Washington: American Historical Association, 1913.

Browne, Robert. *A Book which Showeth the Life and Manners of all True Christians.* Middleburg, Zealand, Denmark: imprinted by Richard Painter, 1582. British Museum.

Bryce, James. *The American Commonwealth.* 2 vols. London and New York: Macmillan Co., 1888.

Brydon, George MacLaren. *Virginia's Mother Church.* Richmond: Virginia Historical Society. Vols. I and II, 1947–1952.

Brynestad, Lawrence E. *The Great Awakening in the New England and Middle Colonies.* Journal of the Presbyterian Historical Society. Vol. 14, No. 2, June 1930; and No. 3, Sept. 1930. Philadelphia.

Buchman, Frank N. D. *Remaking the World.* New York: McBride & Co., 1949. London: Blandford Press, 1953.

Budd, Thomas. *Good Order Established in Pennsylvania and New Jersey.* E. Armstrong, ed. New York: W. Gowans, 1865.

Buffington, Joseph. *The Soul of George Washington.* Philadelphia: Dorrance & Co., 1936.

Burrage, Champlin. *The Early English Dissenters in the Light of Recent Research.* Cambridge, England: Cambridge University Press, 1912.

Butterfield, L. H., ed. *Adams Family Correspondence.* Cambridge: Harvard University Press, 2 vols. published, 1963; 2 vols. published, 1973.

Butterfield, L. H., ed. *Diary and Autobiography of John Adams.* 4 vols. Cambridge: Harvard University Press, 1961.

Callender, John. *Historical Discourse on the Civil and Religious Affairs of the Colony of Rhode Island.* Providence: Knowles, Vose & Co., 1838. (Rhode Island Historical Society Collections, Vol. IV.)

Catton, Bruce. *Centennial History of the Civil War.* 3 vols. Garden City, N.Y.: Doubleday & Co., 1961.

Chatterton, Edward Keble. *Sailing the Seas.* (Life of Columbus.) New York: Chapman, 1931.

Clark, Harry Hayden. *Thomas Paine, Representative Selections.* New York: American Book Co., 1944.

Commager, Henry Steele. *Living Ideas in America.* New York: Harper & Brothers, 1951.

Commins, Saxe. *Basic Writings of George Washington.* New York: Random House, 1948.

Cotton, John. *God's Promise to His Plantations.* London: 1630. Old South Leaflets, Twelfth Series. Boston, Old South Meeting House, 1894.

Crane, Verner W. *Benjamin Franklin's Letters to the Press, 1758–1775.* Chapel Hill: University of North Carolina Press, 1950.

Craven, Wesley F. *The Southern Colonies in the Seventeenth Century, 1607–1689.* Baton Rouge: Louisiana State University Press.

Crouse, Nellis M. *Causes of the Great Migration, 1630–1640.* The New England Quarterly, Vol. V; January 1932. Orono, Maine: The University Press.

Cushing, Harry Alonzo. *The Writings of Samuel Adams.* New York: G. P. Putnam's Sons, 1904–1908.

Davidson, Philby. *Propaganda and the American Revolution.* Chapel Hill: University of North Carolina Press, 1941.

Day, Richard Ellsworth. *Flagellant on Horseback; The Life Story of David Brainerd.* Philadelphia: Judson Press, 1950.

Documents Illustrative of the Formation of the Union of the American States. Washington: U.S. Government Printing Office, 1927.

Donovan, Frank. *The Benjamin Franklin Papers.* New York: Dodd, Mead & Co., 1962.

Ellis, John Harvard, ed. *The Works of Anne Bradstreet.* (Charlestown: A. E. Cutter, 1867.) New York: P. Smith, 1932. (Reprint of 1867 ed.)

Farrand, Max, ed. *The Autobiography of Benjamin Franklin.* Berkeley: University of California Press, 1964.

Ferm, Vergilius, ed. *Puritan Sage, Collected Writings of Jonathan Edwards.* New York: Library Publishers, 1953.

Fitzpatrick, John C., ed. *Writings of Washington.* 39 vols. Washington: U.S. Government Printing Office, 1931–1944.

Foote, Henry W. *Thomas Jefferson, Champion of Religious Freedom, Advocate of Christian Morals.* Boston: Beacon Press, 1947.

Ford, Henry Jones. *The Scotch Irish in America.* Princeton: Princeton University Press, 1915.

Ford, Paul L., ed. *Autobiography of Thomas Jefferson.* New York: G. P. Putnam's Sons, 1914.

Ford, Worthington Chauncey. *Writings of George Washington.* 14 vols. New York: G. P. Putnam's Sons, 1889.

Foxe, John. *Foxe's Book of Martyrs.* (Many editions.) New York: W. Borradaile, 1829; New York, Cincinnati: The Abingdon Press, 1932.

Franklin, Benjamin. *An Historical Review of the Constitution and Government of Pennsylvania.* London: 1759.

Freeman, Douglas Southall. *George Washington, A Biography.* New York: Charles Scribner's Sons, 1948–54. 7 vols.

Gayley, Charles Mills. *Shakespeare and the Founders of Liberty in America.* New York: Macmillan, 1917.

Gewehr, Wesley M. *The Great Awakening in Virginia, 1740–1780.* Durham, N.C.: Duke University Press, 1930.

Gooch, George Peabody. *English Democratic Ideals in the 17th Century.* (Revised by Laski.) New York: Macmillan, 1927.

Gray, Stanley. *The Political Thought of John Winthrop.* New England Quarterly, Vol. III, October, 1930. Orono, Maine: The University Press.

Gurn, Joseph. *Charles Carroll of Carrollton, 1737–1832.* New York: P. J. Kenedy Sons, 1932.

Hacker, Andrew. *The Federalist Papers.* Comprehensive Selection. New York: Washington Square Press, 1964.

Hall, Thomas C. *Religious Background of American Culture.* Boston: Little, Brown & Co., 1930.

Haller, William, ed. *Tracts on Liberty in the Puritan Revolution 1638–1647.* New York: Columbia University Press, 1934.

Haller, William, and Godfrey Davies. *The Leveller Tracts.* New York: Columbia University Press, 1944.

Hanna, Charles A. *The Scotch Irish.* New York: G. P. Putnam's Sons, 1902. 2 vols.

Haraszti, Zoltan. *John Adams and the Prophets of Progress.* Cambridge: Harvard University Press, 1952.

Harnsberger, Caroline T. *A Lincoln Treasury.* Chicago: Wilcox & Follett, 1950.

Harvard Classics, Volume 33. *Voyages and Travels.* New York: Collier & Son, c. 1910.

Heimert, Alan. *Religion and the American Mind.* Cambridge: Harvard University Press.

Hill, John Wesley. *Abraham Lincoln, Man of God.* New York and London: G. P. Putnam's Sons, 1930.

Hirsch, Arthur Henry. *The Huguenots of Colonial South Carolina.* Durham, N.C.: Duke University Press, 1928.

Hogan, John J. *I Am Not Alone.* Mackinac Island, Michigan: Mackinac Press, Bennett Hall, 1947.

Hosmer, James K., ed. *History of New England.* John Winthrop, author. 2 vols. New York: Charles Scribner's Sons, 1908.

Howard, Peter. *Design For Dedication.* Speeches, with foreword by Richard Cardinal Cushing, Archbishop of Boston. Chicago: Henry Regnery Co., 1964.

BIBLIOGRAPHY

Hutchinson, Thomas. *History of the Province of Massachusetts Bay.* 3 vols. Boston: John Fleet, 1765.

Jameson, J. Franklin. *The American Revolution as a Social Movement.* Princeton: Princeton University Press, 1926.

Jefferson, Thomas. *The Life and Morals of Jesus of Nazareth.* Boston: Beacon Press, 1951.

Johnson, Edward. *Wonder-Working Providence of Sion's Saviour in New England.* Andover, Mass.: Warren F. Draper, 1867.

Johnston, Mary. *Pioneers of the Old South.* "The Chronicles of America," Series 5. New Haven: Yale University Press, 1920.

Johnstone, William J. *Abraham Lincoln, The Christian.* New York: The Abingdon Press, 1928.

Johnstone, William J. *George Washington, The Christian.* New York: The Abingdon Press, 1929.

Johnstone, William J. *How Lincoln Prayed.* New York: The Abingdon Press, 1932.

Jones, Rufus M., and others. *The Quakers in the American Colonies.* New York: Macmillan, 1911.

Keyes, Nelson Beecher. *Ben Franklin, An Affectionate Portrait.* Garden City, N.Y.: Hanover House, 1956.

Klett, Guy Soulliard. *Presbyterians in Colonial Pennsylvania.* Philadelphia: University of Pennsylvania Press, 1937.

Koch, Adrienne, and William Peden, eds. *Life and Selected Writings of Thomas Jefferson.* New York: Knopf, 1944.

Koch, Adrienne, and William Peden, eds. *Selected Writings of John Adams and John Quincy Adams.* New York: Knopf, 1946.

Kuhns, Levi Oscar. *The German and Swiss Settlements of Colonial Pennsylvania.* New York: Abingdon Press, 1914.

Labaree, Leonard, and William B. Willcox, eds. *The Papers*

of Benjamin Franklin. New Haven: Yale University Press, 1975. This series is being undertaken by Yale University and the American Philosophical Society. The series has been completed through 1772.

Lawson, John. *History of North Carolina.* (1709) Richmond: Garrett and Massie, 1952.

Ludwig, Emil. *Lincoln.* Boston: Little, Brown & Co., 1930.

MacCracken, Henry Noble. *Prologue to Independence.* New York: James H. Heineman, Inc., 1964.

McGrady, Edward. *The History of South Carolina under the Proprietary Government, 1670–1719.* New York: Macmillan, 1897.

McGrady, Edward. *The History of South Carolina under the Royal Government, 1719–1776.* New York: Macmillan, 1897.

McSherry, James. *A History of Maryland.* Baltimore: Murphy & Co., 1852.

Marsh, Daniel L. *The American Canon.* New York: The Abingdon Press, 1939.

Mather, Cotton. *Magnalia Christi Americana.* Hartford: Silas Andrus, 1820.

Matthews, James McFarlane. *The Bible and Civil Government.* New York: Robert Carter & Brothers, 1850.

Maxson, Charles H. *The Great Awakening in the Middle Colonies.* Chicago: University of Chicago Press, 1920.

Miller, John C. *Origins of the American Revolution.* Boston: Little, Brown & Co., 1943.

Miller, John C. *Sam Adams Pioneer in Propaganda.* Boston: Little, Brown & Co., 1936.

Miller, Perry. *Errand into the Wilderness.* Third Series, Vol. 10, No. 1, January, 1953; William and Mary Quarterly, published by the Institute of Early American History and Culture, Williamsburg, Va.

Miller, Perry. *Jonathan Edwards.* New York: W. Sloane Associates, 1949.

Miller, Perry. *The New England Mind*. New York: Macmillan, 1939.

Miller, Perry. *Orthodoxy in Massachusetts*. Cambridge: Harvard University Press, 1933.

Miller, Perry, and Thomas M. Johnson. *The Puritans*. New York: American Book Co., 1938.

Morgan, Edmund S. *The American Revolution, Two Centuries of Interpretation*. Englewood Cliffs, N.J.: Prentice-Hall.

Morison, Samuel Eliot. *Admiral of the Ocean Sea, A Life of Christopher Columbus*. Boston: Little, Brown & Co., 1942.

Morison, Samuel Eliot. *Sources and Documents Illustrating the American Revolution 1764–1788 and the Formation of the Federal Constitution*. New York: Oxford University Press, 1965.

Morison, Samuel Eliot. *Builders of the Bay Colony*. Boston: Houghton Mifflin, 1930.

Morison, Samuel Eliot. *The Oxford History of the American People*. New York: Oxford University Press, 1965.

Morison, Samuel Eliot. *The Puritan Pronaos*. New York: New York University Press, 1936.

Morison, Samuel Eliot. *Samuel de Champlain, Father of New France*. Boston: Little, Brown & Co., 1972.

Morris, Richard B. *The Basic Ideas of Alexander Hamilton*. New York: Washington Square Press, 1956.

Mowat, R. C. *Climax of History*. London: Blandford Press, 1951.

Murdock, Kenneth B., ed. *Handkerchiefs from Paul*. Cambridge: Harvard University Press, 1927.

Murdock, Kenneth B. *Increase Mather, the Foremost American Puritan*. Cambridge: Harvard University Press, 1925.

Murdock, Kenneth. *Literature and Theology in Colonial New England*. Cambridge: Harvard University Press, 1949.

Murray, John A., ed. *George Washington's Annals of Civility and Decent Behavior.* New York: G. P. Putnam's Sons, 1942.

Murray, John Courtney, S.J. *We Hold These Truths—Catholic Reflections on the American Proposition.* Garden City, N.Y.: Image Books, Doubleday & Co., 1964.

Myers, Albert Cook. *Narratives of Early Pennsylvania, West New Jersey and Delaware.* New York: Charles Scribner's Sons, 1912.

Nagel, Paul C. *One Nation Indivisible—The Union in American Thought 1776–1861.* New York: Oxford University Press, 1964.

Neal, Daniel. *The History of New England.* 2 vols. London: printed for J. Clark, R. Ford and R. Cruttenden, 1720.

The New England Primer. (Many editions.) Boston, New York: Ginn & Co., 1906; or Springfield, Mass.: G & C Merriam Co., 1943.

Nickalls, John L., ed. *Journal of George Fox.* Cambridge, England: Cambridge University Press, 1952.

Nicolay, John George, and John Hay, eds. *Complete Works of Abraham Lincoln.* 12 vols. New York: F. D. Tandy Co., 1905.

Ninde, Edward S. *George Whitefield, Prophet and Preacher.* New York, Cincinnati: Abingdon Press, 1924.

Norton, Thomas James. *The Constitution of the United States—Its Sources and Its Application.* New York: Committee for Constitutional Government, Inc., 1960.

Nuttall, Geoffrey F. *The Holy Spirit in Puritan Faith and Experience.* Oxford: Basil Blackwell, 1946.

Oglethorpe, James Edward. *A New and Accurate Account of the Provinces of South Carolina and Georgia.* London: printed for J. Worrall and sold by J. Roberts, 1732.

Oldroyd, Osborn H. *Words of Lincoln.* Washington: O. H. Oldroyd, 1895.

Padover, Saul K. *Jefferson, A Great American's Life and Ideas.* Abridged by the author. New York and Toronto: Mentor Books, The New American Library, 1952.

Paine, Thomas. *Common Sense.* New York: Rimington & Hooper, 1928.

Parrington, Vernon L. *The Colonial Mind.* Vol. I, "Main Currents in American Thought." New York: Harcourt, Brace & Co., 1927.

Pease, Theodore C. *The Leveller Movement.* Washington: American Historical Association, 1916.

Penn, William. *No Cross, No Crown.* New York: Collins, Brother & Co., 1845.

Perry, William Stevens, ed. *Historical Collections Relating to the American Colonial Church.* Vol. I, "Virginia." Hartford, Conn.: Church Press, 1870.

Prince, Thomas, ed. *The Christian History.* (Magazine, published 1743–1744, Boston.)

Ramsay, David. *History of the American Revolution.* Philadelphia, 1789.

Richardson, James D. *Messages and Papers of the Presidents, 1789–1897.* Washington: U.S. Government Printing Office, 1896–1899.

Rossiter, Clinton Lawrence. *Seedtime of the Republic.* New York: Harcourt, Brace & Co., 1953.

Sachse, Julius Friedrich. *The German Pietists of Provincial Pennsylvania, 1694–1708.* Philadelphia: printed for the author, 1895.

Sandburg, Carl. *Lincoln. The Prairie Years and the War Years.* Reader's Digest Illustrated Edition. New York: Harcourt, Brace, Jovanovich, Inc., 1954.

Saunderson, Henry Hallam. *Puritan Principles and American Ideals.* Boston: Pilgrim Press, 1930.

Schachter, Nathan. *The Founding Fathers.* New York: G. P. Putnam's Sons, 1954.

Schroeder, John Frederick. *The Maxims of Washington.* Mt. Vernon, Va.: Mt. Vernon Ladies' Assn., 1942.

Semple, Robert B. *History of the Rise and Progress of the Baptists in Virginia.* Richmond: Published by the Author, 1810.

Sermons on Sacramental Occasions. By Divers Ministers. Boston: J. Draper for D. Henchman, 1739.

Shepard, Thomas. *Subjection to Christ, in all His Ordinances And Appointments, the Best Means to Preserve our Liberty.* London: J. Rothwell, 1652.

Smith, Samuel. *The History of the Colony of Nova-Caesaria, or New Jersey.* Burlington, N.J.: 1765; Trenton, N.J.: Sharp, 1877.

Sparks, Jared. *Writings of George Washington.* 12 vols. Boston: Little, Brown & Co., 1855.

Stearn, Gerald Emanuel, and Albert Fried, eds. *The Essential Lincoln. Selected Writings.* New York: Crowell Publishing Co., 1962.

Stephenson, George Malcolm. *The Puritan Heritage.* New York: Macmillan, 1952.

Stifler, James M. *The Religion of Benjamin Franklin.* New York, London: D. Appleton & Co., 1925.

Stith, William. *The History of the First Discovery and Settlement of Virginia.* Williamsburg: Printed by William Parks, 1747; New York: Reprinted for Joseph Sabin, 1865.

Stokes, A. P. *Church and State in the United States.* New York: Harper & Brothers, 1950. 2 vols.

Sweet, William Warren. *Religion in Colonial America.* New York: Charles Scribner's Sons, 1949.

Sweet, William Warren. *Religion in the Development of American Culture, 1765–1840.* New York: Charles Scribner's Sons, 1952.

Sweet, William Warren. *The Story of Religions in America.* New York: Harper & Brothers, 1930.

Tansill, Charles Callan, ed. *The Making of the American Republic. The Great Documents, 1774–1789.* New Rochelle, N.Y.: Arlington House.

Tennent, Gilbert. *The Danger of an Unconverted Ministry.* Philadelphia: Benjamin Franklin, 1740.

Tennent, Gilbert. *Discourses on Several Important Subjects.* Philadelphia: W. Bradford, 1745.

Tennent, Gilbert. *Remarks Presented to the Synod of Philadelphia, 1741.* Philadelphia: Printed by Benjamin Franklin.

Thomas, Benjamin P. *Abraham Lincoln.* New York: Alfred Knopf, 1952.

Thomas, Elbert Duncan. *This Nation Under God.* New York: Harper & Brothers, 1950.

Thomson, Rev. J. H. *The Martyr Graves of Scotland.* Edinburgh and London: Anderson & Ferrier.

Tittle, Walter, comp. *Colonial Holidays.* New York: Doubleday, Page & Co., 1910.

Tracy, Joseph. *The Great Awakening.* Boston: Tappan & Dennet, 1842.

Trevitt, Virginia. *The American Heritage—Design for National Character.* Charlotte, Santa Barbara: McNally & Loftin, 1964.

Trinterud, Leonard J. *The Forming of an American Tradition.* Philadelphia: Westminster Press, 1949.

Trumbull, Benjamin. *A Complete History of Connecticut, 1630 to the Close of the Indian Wars.* 2 vols. New Haven: Maltby, Goldsmith & Co., 1818.

Tyerman, L. *Life of George Whitefield.* 2 vols. London: Hodder & Stoughton, 1890.

Tyler, Lyon Gardiner. *Narratives of Early American History Series.* New York: Charles Scribner's Sons, 1907.

Tyler, Moses Coit. *A History of American Literature, 1607–1765.* New York: G. P. Putnam's Sons, c. 1878.

Umbreit, Kenneth Bernard. *Founding Fathers.* New York: Harper & Brothers, 1941.

Van Doren, Carl Clinton, ed. *The Letters of Benjamin Franklin and Jane Mecom*. Princeton: Princeton University Press, 1950.

Van Doren, Mark, ed. *Samuel Sewall's Diary*. New York: Macy-Masins, 1927.

Viles, Jonas. *Letters and Addresses of George Washington*. New York: Unit Book Publishing Co., 1908.

Vrooman, Lee. *The Faith That Built America*. New York: Arrowhead Books, 1955.

Walker, Williston. *Ten New England Leaders*. New York: Silver, Burdett & Co., 1901.

Washburn, Wilcomb E., ed. *The Indian and the White Man*. Garden City, N.Y.: Anchor Books, Doubleday & Co., 1964.

Weeks, Stephen Beauregard. *Religious Development in the Province of North Carolina*. Johns Hopkins University Studies in History and Political Science. 10th Series. Nos. 5–6. Baltimore, 1892.

Wertenbaker, Thomas J. *The Puritan Oligarchy—The Founding of American Civilization*. New York: Charles Scribner's Sons, 1947.

White, Fr. Andrew. "A Briefe Relation of the Voyage unto Maryland, 1634." From *Narratives of Early Maryland*. Hall, Clayton Coleman, ed. New York: Charles Scribner's Sons, 1910.

Whitefield, George. *Eighteen Sermons*. Springfield, Mass.: Thos. Dickman, 1808.

Whitefield, George. *A Select Collection of Letters*. (1734–1770) London: Edward & Charles Dilly, 1772. 3 vols.

Whitefield, George. *Sermons on Various Subjects*. Philadelphia: B. Franklin, 1740.

Whitehead, Alfred North. *The Dialogues of Alfred North Whitehead*. Lucien Price, ed. Boston: Little, Brown & Co., 1954.

Willcox, William B., see Labaree.

Williams, Roger. *Experiments of Spiritual Life and Health.* Winthrop S. Hudson, ed. Philadelphia: Westminster Press, 1951.

Wilstach, Paul, ed. *Correspondence of John Adams and Thomas Jefferson, 1812–1826.* Indianapolis: Bobbs-Merrill Co., 1925.

Winslow, Ola Elizabeth. *Jonathan Edwards. Basic Writings.* New York and Toronto: New American Library, 1966.

Winslow, Ola Elizabeth. *Meeting House Hill, 1630–1783.* New York: Macmillan, 1952.

The Winthrop Papers. 1929, 1931, 1943–4, 4 vols. Boston: The Massachusetts Historical Society.

Wirt, William. *The Life and Character of Patrick Henry.* Philadelphia: Porter & Coates, c. 1832.

Wirt, William. *Patrick Henry; Life, Correspondence and Speeches.* New York: Charles Scribner's Sons, 1891.

Woodhouse, A.S.P., ed. *Puritanism and Liberty, Being the Army Debates (1647–1649).* London: J. M. Dent & Sons, Ltd., 1938.

Woolman, John. *Journal.* Janet Whitney, ed. Chicago: Henry Regnery Co., 1950–51.

Wright, Louis B. *The Cultural Life of the American Colonies, 1607–1763.* New York: Harper & Brothers, 1957.

Wright, Louis B. *Religion and Empire; The Alliance Between Piety and Commerce in English Expansion, 1558–1625.* Chapel Hill: University of North Carolina Press, 1943.

Wroth, L. Kinvin, and Hiller E. Zobel, eds. *Legal Papers of John Adams.* 4 vols. Cambridge: Harvard University Press, 1961.

Zeichner, Oscar. *Connecticut's Years of Controversy, 1750–1776.* Chapel Hill: University of North Carolina Press, 1949.

NOTES

PROLOGUE

1–Great Seal of the United States

2–de Crèvecoeur, Hector St. John—*Letters of an American Farmer*—1782

PREFACE

1–Emerson, Ralph Waldo—*Address before the Phi Beta Kappa Society, Cambridge, Mass.*—1837

2–Paine, Thomas—*The American Crisis*—1776

3–Massachusetts Church Assembly—Message to the General Court—1679

4–Columbus, Christopher—Letter to Luis de Santangel—1493

5–Jefferson, Thomas—Letter to John Tyler—May 26, 1810

CHAPTER I

1–Adams, John—*Dissertation on the Canon and Feudal Law*—Aug., 1765

2–Plymouth Plantation—Commission for Regulating Plantations—1634

3–King James I—Statement to Conference at Hampton Court—Jan. 14, 1604–1605

4–Inscription, Martyrs' Monument—Glasgow Cathedral

5–Bradford, William—*History of Plimoth Plantation*, Chapter I

6–Miller, Perry—*Errand into the Wilderness*, p. 14

CHAPTER II

1–Winthrop, John—Sermon, *A Model of Christian Charity* (on board the "Arbella"), June 12, 1630

2–Adams, John Quincy—Statement on the Mayflower Pact, 1802

3–Robinson, Rev. John—Letter to Sir Edwin Sandys—Dec. 15, 1617

4–Browne, Rev. Robert—*A Book which Showeth the Life and Manners of all True Christians*—1582

5–Winthrop, John—Ibid.

6–Exeter, New Hampshire—"Compact"—July 14, 1639

7–Rhode Island—Colonial Charter—July 18, 1663

8–West New Jersey—Message from the Proprietors to the Quaker Colony—1676

9–Connecticut—"Fundamental Orders"—Jan. 24, 1639

10–New England Confederation—Preamble to Constitution—May 19, 1643

11–Massachusetts General Court—"Body of Liberties"—1641

12–Gilbert, Sir Humphrey—Charter from Queen Elizabeth I—1582

13–Massachusetts Bay Colony Assembly—Declaration, quoted, S. E. Morison, *The Oxford History of the American People*, p. 13.

14–Cotton, Rev. John—quoted by Perry Miller, *The New England Mind*, p. 410

15–Lincoln, Abraham—Speech, 1848, quoted, *Alistair Cooke's America*, p. 214

16–Adams, John—Letter to Thomas Jefferson—May 29, 1818

Chapter III

1–Virginia-London Company—Eye-Witness Account of Landing at Jamestown—April 26, 1607

2–Gilbert, Sir Humphrey—*Voyage to Newfoundland*—1583

3–Virginia-London Company—Report, *A True Declaration of the Colonie in Virginia*—1610

4–Smith, Captain John—quoted, S. E. Morison, Ibid. p. 52

5–Virginia-London Company—Charter of 1606

6–Sandys, Sir Edwin—Virginia-London Company, Ibid.

7–Virginia, Royal Province of—"Articles" agreed on and

concluded at James City in Virginia—Mar. 12, 1651

8–Crashaw, William—*Address before Lord de la Warr and the Virginia-London Company*—Feb. 1610

9–Virginia-London Company—*"Nova Britannia"*—1610

10–Idem—*Articles, Instructions and Orders*

11–Idem—*Minutes of the First Assembly*, Jamestown, August 9–14, 1619

12–Idem—Broadside—*Offering most excellent fruits by planting in Virginia*—1610

13–Hammond, John—*Leah and Rachel*—1656

14–Rolfe, John—Letter to Deputy-Governor, Sir Thomas Dale—1614

15–Lawson, John—*A New Voyage to the Carolinas*—1709

16–Georgia—Charter, June 20, 1732 (granted by King George II)

Chapter IV

1–New Haven Compact—"Fundamental Articles"—June 4, 1639

2–Smith, Captain John—*Description of New England*—1616

3–Morison, Samuel Eliot—Ibid. p. 61

4–Miller, Perry—Ibid. p. 416

5–Johnson, Rev. Edward—*Wonder-working Providence of Sion's Saviour in New England*—1654

6–Bradford, William—Ibid.

7–Williams, Roger—Letter to the Town of Providence—Jan. 1654–55

8–Paine, Thomas—*Observations on the Rights of Man*—1791–92

9–White, Rev. John—*Planter's Plea*, quoted, *New England Quarterly*, Vol. V, Jan.-Oct. 1932, p. 26

10–Dudley, Governor Joseph—Letter to the Countess of Lincoln, Mar. 20, 1630

11–Massachusetts Bay Colony Council—Letter to the Lords and Gentlemen, etc. 1636

12–Winthrop, John—Ibid.

13–Continental Congress—Ordinance for Ascertaining the Mode of Disposing of Lands in the Western Territory —May 20, 1785

14–Massachusetts Bay—Colonists' Letter—"Certain Proposals made by Lord Saye and Sele, Lord Brooke, etc. with the Answers Thereto"—March 1636

15–Massachusetts Bay Colony Council—Ibid.

16–Danforth, Samuel—*An Almanack for the Year of Our Lord 1648*

CHAPTER V

1–Penn, William—Sermon, *No Cross, No Crown*—1669

2–Ibid.

3–West New Jersey—Ibid.

4–Pennsylvanians—"One of the first," quoted, L. Vrooman, *The Faith That Built America*, p. 65

5–Penn, William—Statement, 1682, quoted, Ibid.

6–Idem—Preface to "Frame of Government of Pennsylvania"—1682

7–Idem—Pennsylvania "Charter of Liberties"—1701

8–Zimmerman, John Jacob—from Berard Groese of Amsterdam, *Historia Quakeriana*—1697

9–McClure, David—Diary, Sat., April 24th, 1772

10–White, Father Andrew—*A Briefe Relation of the Voyage into Maryland*—1634

11–Calvert, Cecelius, Lord Baltimore—Oath prescribed for all Maryland Governors—1636

12–Calvert, Charles, Lord Baltimore—Message to the Privy Council—1677

13–Ibid.

14–King's College, New York—Public Prospectus, 1774— Sections III, IV, V

CHAPTER VI

1–Roosevelt, Franklin D.—quoted, L. Vrooman, Ibid. p. 69

2–Morison, Samuel Eliot—Ibid. pp. 150–51

3–Connecticut General Assembly—"Recommendations"—
1675

4–Edwards, Jonathan—*A Treatise Concerning Religious Affections*—1746

5–Edwards, Jonathan—*Thoughts on the Revival of Religion in New England*, 1740

6–Ibid.

7–Ninde, Edward S.—*George Whitefield, Prophet and Preacher*, p. 173

8–Smith, Rev. Joseph—Sermon, *The Character of Whitefield*—Charleston, South Carolina, 1749

9–Whitefield, George—*Journal*—1740

10–Franklin, Benjamin—*Autobiography*

11–Tennent, Rev. Gilbert—*The Righteousness of the Scribes and Pharisees*—Remarks upon a Protestation (printed by Benjamin Franklin)

12–Trumbull, Rev. Benjamin—*History of Connecticut to 1764*

13–Heimert, Alan—*Religion and the American Mind*, p. 15

14–Gewehr, Wesley M.—*The Great Awakening in Virginia*, p. 218

15–Heimert, Alan—Ibid.

16–de Tocqueville, Alexis—*De La Démocratie en Amérique*—1835

Chapter VII

1–Whitehead, Alfred North—*The Dialogues of Alfred North Whitehead*

2–Franklin, Benjamin—*Autobiography*

3–Adams, John—*Novanglus, or a History of the Dispute with America from its Origin to the Present Time*—1774

4–Otis, James—*A Vindication of the Conduct of the House of Representatives of the Province of Massachusetts Bay, etc.*—1762

5–Willard, Rev. Samuel—Election Address, Old South Church, Boston, May 30, 1694

6–Pemberton, Rev. Ebenezer—Election Address, Massachusetts, 1710

7–Bulkley, Rev. John—Election Address, Connecticut—1713

8–Alison, Rev. Francis—Essay, *Of the Rights of Ye Supreme Power and Ye Methods of Acquiring It*—1756

9–Hamilton, Alexander—*The Farmer Refuted, a full Vindication of the Measures of Congress, etc.*—Feb. 5, 1775

10–Cromwell, Oliver—Letter, Sept. 1643—from *Letters and Speeches of Oliver Cromwell*, ed. Carlyle

11–Ramsey, David—*History of the American Revolution* —1789

12–Mason, George—Robin vs. Hardway—I Jefferson 109, 1772

13–Declaration of Independence—Preamble—July 4, 1776

14–Ibid.

Chapter VIII

1–Adams, John—*Some Thoughts on Government*—Jan., 1776

2–Paine, Thomas—Ibid., 1793

3–Henry, Patrick—Speech, Virginia House of Burgesses— Mar. 23, 1775

4–Adams, John—Speech, Continental Congress, Philadelphia—1776

5–Hamilton, Alexander—Letter to Robert Morris—Aug. 13, 1782

6–Jefferson, Thomas—Letter to George Washington—Apr. 13, 1784

7–Lincoln, Abraham—Speech, Independence Hall, Philadelphia—Feb. 22, 1861

8–Jefferson, Thomas—*Notes on Virginia*—1782

9–Trumbull, Jonathan—Proclamation—June 16, 1776

10–Hamilton, Alexander—Letter to "Concerned Citizens," New York—1784

11–Washington, George—At the Constitutional Convention, Philadelphia—1787

12–Madison, James—*The Federalist*, No. 37

13–Bryce, James—*The American Commonwealth*—1888, i, 25

14–Jefferson, Thomas—Letter to James Madison—Nov. 18, 1788

15–Dickinson, John—*Political Writings*, quoted, M. C. Tyler, *Literary History of the American Revolution*, i, 48

16–Jefferson, Thomas—Letter to Col. William Duane—Mar. 28, 1811

17–Adams, John—First Inaugural Address—Mar. 4, 1797

18–Adams, John—Letter to Josiah Quincy—Feb. 9, 1811

19–Hamilton, Alexander—*The Federalist*, No. 22

20–Jefferson, Thomas—*Notes on Virginia*—1774

21–Jefferson, Thomas—Letter to Samuel Adams—Feb. 26, 1800

22–Jefferson, Thomas—Letter to James Madison—Jan. 30, 1787

23–Adams, John—*Diary*—Wed., May 6, 1778

24–Adams, John—Letter to Mercy Warren—Apr. 16, 1776

25–Bryce, James—Ibid., ii, 450–51

26–Evans, Rev. Israel—Sermon, Easton, Pennsylvania—Oct., 1779

27–Morris, Gouverneur—Letter to George Washington—1782, quoted, Theodore Roosevelt, *Gouverneur Morris*

28–Adams, John—*Novanglus, etc.*—1774

29–Adams, John—Letter to Benjamin Rush—Sept. 27, 1808

30–Trumbull, Jonathan—Letter to Silas Deane—Oct. 6, 1778

31–Henry, Patrick—Letter to A. Blair—Jan. 8, 1779

32–Washington, George—Letter to the Hebrew Congregation, Savannah, Georgia—May, 1790

33–Penn, William—Preface to "Frame of Government of Pennsylvania"—1682

34–Jefferson, Thomas—Letter to J. Fishback—1809

35–Franklin, Benjamin—Letter to Dr. Samuel Johnson—Aug. 23, 1750

36–Adams, Samuel—Letter to James Warren—Dec. 26, 1775

37–Ibid.

38–Jefferson, Thomas—"Opinion"—Apr. 28, 1793

39–Jefferson, Thomas—Letter to J. Fishback

40–University of Virginia—"Aim and Curriculum, etc."—Aug. 4, 1818

41–University of Virginia—Report of the Commissioners—Aug., 1818

42–Otis, James—*The Rights of the British Colonies Asserted and Proved*

43–Adams, John—Letter to his grandson, George Washington Adams (in St. Petersburg, Russia)—Sept. 15, 1811

44–Adams, John—*Diary*, June 14, 1756

CHAPTER IX

1–Adams, Abigail—Statement, quoted, D. S. Freeman—*George Washington*, VII, App. 3, p. 648

2–Jefferson, Thomas—Letter to Walter Jones—Jan. 2, 1814

3–Freeman, Douglas Southall—Ibid., vii, xxiv

4–Davies, Rev. Samuel—Sermon to the Militia, Hanover County, Virginia—Aug., 1758

5–Washington, George—Quoted by D. S. Freeman—Ibid., ii, 261

6–Washington, George—Quoted by John Adams, *Diary*—Aug. 31, 1774

7–Henry, Patrick—Statement on Washington—1775

8–Washington, George—Letter to his mother—Sept. 30, 1757

9–Freeman, Douglas Southall—Ibid., i, 383–84

10–Washington, George—Letter to John Augustine Washington—Mar. 25, 1775

11–Adams, John—Letter to Abigail—May, 1775

12–Freeman, Douglas Southall—Ibid., ii, xxiv

13–Ibid.

14–Washington, George—Address to his Officers—Mar. 15, 1783. (From Major Shaw's Journal)

15–Freeman, D. S.—Ibid, iii, xiii, quoting Mark 9, 35

16–Madison, James—Letter to Thomas Jefferson—Jan. 9, 1785

17–Washington, George—To the Constitutional Convention, Philadelphia—1787. Reported by Gouverneur Morris

18–Jefferson, Thomas—Letter to Francis Hopkinson—Mar. 13, 1789

19–Jefferson, Thomas—Letter to George Washington—May 23, 1792

20–Washington, George—Letter to Alexander Hamilton, quoted, D. S. Freeman, Ibid., v, 440

21–Bancroft, George—*History of the Colonization of America*, vii, 398

22–Washington, George—Letter to Jonathan Trumbull—July 20, 1788

23–Lewis, Robert—quoted by Jared Sparks, *Writings of George Washington*, xii, 407

24–Lee, Colonel Henry—"Resolutions"—Dec. 19, 1799

Chapter X

1–La Rochefoucauld-Liancourt, Duc de—*Voyage dans les Etats-Unis d'Amérique*—1799

2–Adams, John—*Novanglus, etc.*—1775

3–Adams, John—*Dissertation on the Canon and Feudal Law*—Aug., 1765

4–Adams, John—*Autobiography*

5–Ibid.

6–Stockton, Richard—Statement, quoted, J. M. Anderson, *Adams and Jefferson—The Story of a Friendship*

7–Jefferson, Thomas—quoted, Daniel Webster, Speech, Faneuil Hall, Boston—Aug. 2, 1826

8–Rush, Dr. Benjamin—Letter to Richard Price—1787

9–Adams, John—Letter to Richard Henry Lee—Nov. 15, 1775

10–Marshall, John—*Life of Washington*

11–Adams, John—First Inaugural Address—Mar. 4, 1797

12–Adams, John—Letter to Mercy Warren—Jan. 8, 1776

13–Adams, John—*Diary*—June 2, 1778

14–Adams, John—Letter to Abigail—Oct. 29, 1775

15–Adams, Abigail—Letter to John—Nov. 5, 1775

16–Adams, Abigail—Letter to John—Nov. 25, 1782

17–Adams, John—Letter to Abigail—May 17, 1776

18–Adams, John—Letter to Abigail—Feb. 10, 1795

19–Adams, Abigail—Letter to John—May 18, 1778

20–Adams, Abigail—Letter to John—Dec. 23, 1782

CHAPTER XI

1–Lincoln, Abraham—Message to Jefferson Birthday Festival—Apr. 6, 1859

2–Jefferson, Thomas—Letter to Benjamin Rush—Sept. 23, 1800. These words are inscribed on the Jefferson Memorial in Washington.

3–Burke, Edmund—*Speech on Conciliation with America* —Mar. 22, 1775

4–Jefferson, Thomas—Letter to Edward Rutledge—July 14, 1787

5–Jefferson, Thomas—*Notes on Virginia*

6–Jefferson, Thomas—Letter to George Washington—Jan. 4, 1786

7–Washington, George—Letter to Thomas Jefferson—July 7, 1781

8–Webster, Daniel—Statement, quoted, *American Historical Report*—1896

9–Hamilton, Alexander—To the Constitutional Convention, Philadelphia—1787 (Yates' Notes)

10–Jefferson, Thomas—Letter to John Adams—Oct. 28, 1813

11–Jefferson, Thomas—Letter to Rev. James Madison— Oct. 28, 1787

12–Jefferson, Thomas—Letter to daughter, Martha—Mar. 28, 1787

13–Jefferson, Thomas—Letter to daughter, Martha—Apr. 7, 1787

14–Jefferson, Thomas—Letter to Peter Carr—Aug. 19, 1785

15–Jefferson, Thomas—Letter to Thomas Jefferson Smith —Feb. 21, 1825

16–Jefferson, Thomas—*Declaration of the Causes and Necessity of Taking Up Arms*—July 6, 1775

17–Jefferson, Thomas—Second Inaugural Address—Mar. 4, 1805

CHAPTER XII

1–Jefferson, Thomas—Letter to Samuel Smith—1798, quoted, S. Padover, *The Complete Jefferson*

2–Franklin, Benjamin—*Autobiography*, quoted, *Harvard Classics*

3–Franklin, Benjamin—*Observations on Reading History* —May 9, 1731

4–Franklin, Benjamin—*Autobiography*, quoted, *Harvard Classics*, i, 79–80

5–Franklin, Benjamin—*Autobiography*, quoted, Ibid., i, 88

6–Franklin, Benjamin—Preface to pamphlet on Smallpox Inoculation, by Dr. William Heberden—1759

7–Franklin, Benjamin—*The Interests of Great Britain Considered, etc.*—Apr., 1760

8–Franklin, Benjamin—Letter to the *Federal Gazette*, Philadelphia—Apr. 8, 1788

9–Darwin, Erasmus—Letter to Benjamin Franklin—1787

10–Hume, David—Letter to Benjamin Franklin, quoted, Bigelow, ed., *The Complete Works of Benjamin Franklin*, iii, 190

11–Franklin, Benjamin—Letter to David Hartley (the younger)—Dec. 5, 1789

12–Franklin, Benjamin—Letter to friends in England— 1787, quoted, C. D. Bowen, *Miracle at Philadelphia*, p. 281

13–Franklin, Benjamin—Letter to Jonathan Shipley, Bishop of St. Asaph's—Feb. 24, 1786

Chapter XIII

1–Whitman, Walt—quoted by A. T. Rice, *Reminiscences of Abraham Lincoln, etc.*

2–Hanks, John—quoted by Emil Ludwig, *Lincoln*, p. 32

3–Lincoln, Abraham—Letter to Joshua Speed—Aug. 24, 1855

4–Lincoln, Abraham—Speech, Springfield, Illinois—June 16, 1858

5–Seward, William Henry—Speech, Rochester, N.Y.—Oct. 25, 1858

6–Lincoln, Abraham—Conversation with Joseph Gillespie, quoted, Emil Ludwig, Ibid., p. 252

7–Lincoln, Abraham—Second Inaugural Address—Mar. 4, 1865

8–Lincoln, Abraham—quoted by J. W. Hill, *Abraham Lincoln, Man of God*

9–Lincoln, Abraham—Speech, Springfield, Illinois—Feb. 11, 1861

10–Lincoln, Abraham—General Order to the Army and Navy—Nov. 15, 1862

11–Lincoln, Abraham—Letter to Horace Greeley—Aug. 22, 1862

12–Lincoln, Abraham—Speech, Peoria, Illinois—Oct. 16, 1854

13–Lincoln, Abraham—First Inaugural Address—Mar. 4, 1861

14–Lincoln, Abraham—Thanksgiving Day Proclamation—Oct. 20, 1864

15–Lincoln, Abraham—To General George C. Meade—July 4, 1863

16–Lincoln, Abraham—Second Inaugural Address—Mar. 4, 1865

17–Jefferson, Thomas—Letter to John Holmes—Apr. 22, 1820

NOTES

18–Lincoln, Abraham—Letter to General U. S. Grant—July
   13, 1863
19–Lincoln, Abraham—Letter to General David Hunter—
   1861
20–Lincoln, Abraham—Quoted by Emil Ludwig, *Lincoln*
21–Lincoln, Abraham—Letter to Mrs. Lydia Bixby—Nov.
   21, 1864
22–Lincoln, Abraham—Quoted by Emil Ludwig, *Lincoln*

CONCLUSION

1–Declaration of Independence—Preamble
2–Morison, Samuel Eliot—*Oxford History of the American People*, p. 223
3–Rush, Dr. Benjamin—Letter to Richard Price—May 25,
   1786
4–Paine, Thomas—*The American Crisis*—1776
5–Washington, George—Letter to Charles Armand-Tuffin,
   Marquis de la Roveria—Oct. 7, 1785
6–Adams, John—Letter to Thomas Jefferson—Aug. 24,
   1815
7–Adams, John—Letter to Hezekiah Niles—Feb. 13, 1818
8–Buchman, Frank N. D.—Speech, Mackinac Conference,
   Michigan—June, 1957
9–Macaulay, Thomas Babington—Letter to Henry S.
   Randall—May 23, 1857
10–Ramsay, David—Ibid.
11–Truman, Senator Harry S.—Speech on occasion of presentation of Moral Re-Armament industrial drama, *The Forgotten Factor*, Philadelphia—Nov. 19, 1943

EPILOGUE

1–Great Seal of the United States
2–Paine, Thomas—*Observations on the Rights of Man*—
   1792–93

APPENDIX

1–Franklin, Benjamin—Letter to Edward Bridgen—Oct.
   2, 1779

167

NOTES

2–Whitefield, George—"A Farmer's Unvarnished Account," quoted, W. W. Sweet, *Religion in Colonial America*, p. 235

3–Madison, James—*The Federalist*, No. 37

4–Morison, Samuel Eliot—*Sources and Documents Illustrating the American Revolution—1764–1788, etc.*

INDEX

Library of Congress Cataloging in Publication Data

Bradley, Francis, 1903-
    The American proposition.

    Bibliography: p.
    Includes index.
        1.   United States—Civilization—To 1783.   2.   United
States—Civilization—1783-1848.   3.   Statesmen—United
States—Biography.   4.   Presidents—United States—
Biography.   5.   National characteristics, American.
    I.   Title.
E162.B77   973'.0992   77-10293